20 · VII · 83

To Mummy

(1983) £5-50

Happy Birthday

with much love

Polly.

THE
PICNIC
PAPERS

THE PICNIC PAPERS

EDITED AND COMPILED BY

Susanna Johnston and Anne Tennant

HUTCHINSON
London Melbourne Sydney Auckland Johannesburg

Hutchinson & Co. (Publishers) Ltd

An imprint of the Hutchinson Publishing Group

17-21 Conway Street, London W1P 6JD

Hutchinson Group (Australia) Pty Ltd
30-32 Cremorne Street, Richmond South, Victoria 3121
PO Box 151, Broadway, New South Wales 2007

Hutchinson Group (NZ) Ltd
32-34 View Road, PO Box 40-086, Glenfield, Auckland 10

Hutchinson Group (SA) Pty Ltd
PO Box 337, Bergvlei 2012, South Africa

Set in VIP Baskerville by D. P. Media Limited,
Hitchin, Hertfordshire

Printed in Great Britain by The Anchor Press Ltd
and bound by Wm Brendon & Son Ltd,
both of Tiptree, Essex

British Library Cataloguing in Publication Data

The Picnic papers.
  1. Picnicking
  I. Johnston, Susanna   II. Tennant, Anne
  642'.3   TX823

ISBN 0 09 152220 X

To our children, who have been out with us
in all sorts of weather

Contents

Introduction

Naturally, our undiluted gratitude goes to the distinguished contributors who have generously shared their picnicking experiences with us in the pages of this book. Each and every one has given such encouragement by their enthusiasm and interest that the pleasure of corresponding, planning and talking with them over the venture has been intense.

We have both been dedicated picnickers since early youth and consequently find the subject of outdoor eating wholly absorbing. After all it is a well-established habit. Our Stone Age forbears could be said to have picnicked after a fashion as they applied flint to firewood, culled berries, or sat with mammoth ribs in hand at the mouth of a cave; but whereas for them there was no alternative, for us there is all the excitement of the break away from daily ritual as we set out to find the perfect place to unpack the basket and perhaps even to find on-the-spot food to add to our provisions.

So – what is a picnic? The *Oxford English Dictionary* tells us in a few lines:

Picnic Originally a fashionable and social entertainment in which each person present contributed a share of the provisions; now, a pleasure party including an excursion to some spot in the country where all partake of a repast out of doors. . . . The essential feature was formerly the individual contribution; now it is the *al fresco* form of the repast.

Picnics, if the *Oxford English Dictionary* is to be trusted, were originally a foreign institution – an institution peculiar to the upper class; the

Annual Register in 1802 declares that 'the rich have their sport, their balls, their parties of pleasure and their *pic-nics*' – and a year or two later James Beresford, in his popular work *The Miseries of Human Life, or the last Groans of Timothy Testy and Samuel Sensitive, with a few supplementary sighs from Mrs Testy*, describes one of his female characters as being 'full of Fete and Picnic and Opera'.

During the last hundred years or so picnicking has become such a popular pleasure that the phrase 'this is no picnic' is an accepted idiom to describe an unpleasant or unpopular experience.

One of the joys of picnicking is proving how much depends on the setting and, cliché though it is, how much better something very ordinary can taste when eaten out of doors. In a bluebell wood with a camp fire blazing, try making a dough of flour and water, add a pinch of salt and nothing else whatsoever. Roll it into a messy ball. Squeeze this lump onto the end of a long pointed stick. Thrust it into the flames and wait for it to turn brown. Here you have a 'damper' – the time-honoured picnic delicacy. It is unlikely that it would be equally appreciated if served at a dining-room table by candlelight.

The very suggestion of a picnic tends to produce a strong reaction. Some people loathe them. Sir Steven Runciman, the historian, would certainly appear to disagree with the modern idea of picnicking as an enjoyable pastime. He tells us in a letter,

Memories crowd up of depression and discomfort; not quite dispelled by a picnic with Agatha Christie on Dartmoor, at which we drank champagne from silver goblets. Nor have my picnics been really eventful. I remember once picnicking on a Syrian roadside with a local colonel who had been sent to accompany me because I insisted on visiting a crusader castle near the Israeli frontier. Poor portly man, he had to climb to a mountaintop with me. And when we paused on the way back to eat, the Israelis took potshots at us from across the frontier, and the colonel, good Muslim though he was, consoled himself with the wine (local and awful) that I had brought with me. There was an earlier picnic with Michael Grant, on top of the Zigana Pass in eastern Turkey, where we had to abandon our food because of the stench of the Turkish army as it passed by, that hot noonday, on its way to liquidate the Kurds. Or again, a picnic organized in Jericho (in 1931) by Abdul Hamid's retired astrologer, where Susanna's grandmother and I were poisoned. I have picnicked in a snowstorm on the Great Wall of China. In 1931, I picnicked more happily, with a Rumanian prince on the (then) Bessarabian frontier, looking at suspicious Russian sentries across the river Dniester. That was happier, as was a picnic on a barge on the river

Mekong where the royal Siamese band played Mozart. But on the whole my experiences have been a trifle *triste*.

However miserable the author of this letter may have been at the time of these ordeals, there can be no denying that his experiences were colourful.

Some people feel that picnics are all very well when necessary, provided they are permitted to stick to the smudgy jam sandwich, hard-boiled egg and bakelite teacup of their youth. We both look back on this type of picnic with nostalgia but never attempt to repeat it.

Some of those who have contributed to this book, Sir Harold Acton, for example, who was the first person to encourage us in this venture, have described unexpected and often nerve-racking adventures that have come about as the result of setting out on a picnic instead of allowing oneself to be securely tethered to a dining room or restaurant table. Some have shown how a day out of doors can be far more entertaining and educative, not to mention beneficial to one's purse, than one in a crowded pub.

Whatever our attitude, it remains a fact that we English have an irresistible habit of eating al fresco, in spite of our unreliable climate. We will eat anywhere, in swamps, on haystacks, in sunshine, hail, fog or drizzle – anything to escape the routine of the kitchen table. Long may the habit last! It is one of our national eccentricities. Not that we can claim the habit as uniquely ours or hail it as something new. This point is underlined by William Rees-Mogg in *The Risen Christ*: 'If he were a human myth he would surely have acted with more sense of occasion, and would be resurrected in the grand style. . . . Instead, two lighter sides of his human character come to the fore, his love of picnics and his ironic sense of humour.'

Now, finally we would like to thank both Anne Allen-Stevens and Clara Johnston, who have typed out the manuscript with great patience; also John Sparrow, who has given much help and encouragement and who suggested the title of *The Picnic Papers*. We have collected photographs from various different sources and would like to thank the many people, Milton Gendel in particular, who have taken so much trouble on our behalf over this.

Proceeds will go to the Stars' Organisation for Spastics and the Glyndebourne Trust.

A Picnic at the Ming Tombs

HAROLD ACTON

The Tuscan countryside has been amenable to picnics since the fifteenth century, when Lorenzo the Magnificent invited his cronies to rustic repasts in the bosky Mugello and in cool Camaldoli. Cured ham and pungent cheese stimulated a thirst for the vintages celebrated in Francesco Redi's dithyrambic *Bacchus in Tuscany*, which in turn stimulated a flow of rhyme and melody. Lorenzo's best poems are redolent of picnics.

The more refined cakes and sandwiches of my childhood were consumed with appetites sharpened by climbs up Vincigliata or Monte Morello and by games of hide-and-seek and blind man's buff, but I remember the delicious cakes better than the company. We lounged on the grass as in Manet's *Déjeuner sur l'herbe*, though none of the girls reclined naked in our midst, for we were strictly supervised by a governess. Since nothing more sensational occurred than a bleeding nose or a bruised knee my memory of those bygone picnics is hazy.

The neighbourhood of Peking, where I spent seven happy years, was even more amenable to picnics. A novel called *Peking Picnic* was popular at the period, but I forget if the title was justified by the contents. Picnics, however, were traditional in ancient China, whose greatest poets considered wine essential to the enjoyment of nature. Many a Chinese scroll depicts parties of poetical tipplers in a secluded spot among mountains and bamboo groves.

The Western Hills near Peking were often chosen for al fresco meals, but after the Japanese invasion it was deemed foolhardy to

venture far from the city, since roving bandits and marauding sol-
diery infested the countryside. The Ming Tombs, for instance,
twenty miles north-west of Peking, were officially out of bounds.

A spirited American lady whom I shall call 'Mrs Schooner' was
determined to take the risk before returning to Massachusetts, and
she invited me to join her for a picnic at the Tombs, perhaps because
she could find no other escort. She told me she had hired a motor car
with some difficulty by paying the driver through the nose. 'He's a
cutie but he's kinda yaller. He was even scared of taking me to the
Summer Palace.'

Unwilling to appear pusillanimous, I agreed to acompany her to
the Valley of Thirteen Tombs. She knew no Chinese, whereas I was
fairly fluent in the language. Though she was double my age she had
twice my energy: her enthusiasm for everything she saw was infec-
tious. The hired car was filled with a rich variety of edibles from the
Hôtel de Pékin where she was staying. She told me she was bringing
foie gras as well as smoked eel and half a dozen bottles of Pouilly. 'I
won't let you starve, dear. You are a good sport to keep me company.
All the others I invited made some lame excuse, the darned cissies!'

Mrs Schooner whooped with laughter as we set off from the hotel.
'Wouldn't it be fun if we were kidnapped by bandits?' she said gaily.
She was dressed and made up as for a morning's shopping in Bond
Street – an invitation to rapine, I thought, in spite of her certain age.
The road was so bumpy that she clung to me when we swerved past a
file of camels. By fits and starts she related her life history. 'At high
school I was a champion wrestler and I've had four husbands to
wrestle with. None of them gave me the love a girl expects: they
were more interested in my dollars. I had a hunch that I'd find my
fifth in China, that's why I'm here. So far nothin' doin'. . . .' About
the idiosyncrasies of her international boyfriends she was embarrass-
ingly candid, but she had never experimented with an Oriental and
she thought it might be worth trying. 'I guess they've a variety of love
tricks but I'm conservative in that department.'

She talked so much that I was distracted from the scenery – a
sweeping bare plain dotted with burial mounds and an occasional
stele. The October weather was serene, the sky like Venetian glass.

After an hour my hostess said, 'I'm getting thirsty, dear, what
about you? Let's stop the car for a nip of dry martini. It's in the big
thermos flask.' So the driver stopped near a file of donkeys, loaded
with panniers and bundled blue figures on top of them. Nothing if

not democratic, she filled a glass for the driver, but he said '*Pu kan*' ('I dare not'), so she offered him some chewing gum and swallowed his portion herself.

Apart from the donkeys the road was deserted. 'How far have we still to go? For twenty miles it seems more like a hundred. I'm glad I brought plenty of nourishment.'

I heartily agreed, for her incessant monologue had become wearisome. The car jogged along almost as slowly as the donkeys and by the time we approached a white marble *p'ai-lou*, or ceremonial gateway, Mrs Schooner announced, 'I'm famished. Let's hop out and eat!' As a magnificent pavilion was visible yonder I proposed that we should stop there. It contained a huge stone tortoise supporting a memorial tablet. Its massive coral-red walls and yellow-tiled double roof against a background of rippling lapis lazuli hills were as impressive as any in the Forbidden City.

'Okay,' said Mrs Schooner. We spread a rug on a patch of coarse grass and unpacked the baskets of victuals with enough glasses and cutlery for at least half a dozen people. 'The situation is pretty but it sure is lonesome,' Mrs Schooner remarked, peering through her binoculars.

'Well, what did you expect? This is where the Ming emperors of the last truly Chinese dynasty were buried with their wives and concubines.'

'It doesn't look like a cemetery to me. Have we come to the right place?'

Certainly the Valley of Thirteen Tombs had nothing akin to the cluttered cemeteries of Europe and America. It was all too grandiose: its monumental buildings were still brightly coloured though decayed, and the landscape was on too vast a scale. No soul was in sight. One was reminded of the Egyptian pyramids and of Shelley's 'Ozymandias': 'Look on my works, ye Mighty, and despair!'

'I guess I'd have liked to be an imperial concubine,' Mrs Schooner mused aloud. 'They must have had loads of fun without responsibilities.'

'I doubt it, for they had jealous wives to contend with. Many were poisoned or drowned in wells.'

'Don't talk of poison, this pâté's yummy. A pity we can't make toast here. Just spread it on a cracker.'

While I was drawing the cork from a bottle of wine three ragged men with guns appeared suddenly from nowhere. 'Bandits,' said our terrified driver and scampered off. The men sauntered up and stared at us while we were eating. They stared as if they had never seen 'foreign devils' before. Robust, with high cheekbones and ruddy complexions, they were typical northerners of peasant stock. 'I guess the boys are hungry,' Mrs Schooner remarked. 'Hi there!' she called, offering them in dumb show some of our chicken and ham and buttered rolls. 'Ask them to sit down and introduce themselves.'

When I spoke to them their faces lit up with broad grins. They sat cross-legged beside us with their battered guns, and once they had sampled our fare they ate like ravenous tigers. Our knives and forks perplexed them; accustomed to chopsticks, they preferred to eat with their fingers. They dangled the layers of fat on the ham above their open mouths and swallowed with a noise of trickling water. Their fingernails were long and black but their teeth were surprisingly clean. 'They have so little hair on their chins that they don't need a shave, but if they had a good wash they'd be quite presentable,' said Mrs Schooner.

Though they were not very communicative, I gathered that they were disbanded soldiers, irregulars who had been fighting the Japanese, whom they ironically referred to as 'dwarf bandits'. Now they intended to make their way home to villages in the north. Concerning ourselves they were inquisitive. 'How old are you? Are you husband and wife? Where do you come from and what is your honourable country?' – the usual questions. Our wine had less appeal for them than the cocktails, but they soon polished off the food. Not a scrap was left for our driver. 'Serve him darn well right for leaving us in the lurch!' was Mrs Schooner's comment.

'*Tsamen tou shih p'êng-yu*' ('We're all friends'), the men repeated, and they belched appreciatively. One of them, flushed with dry martinis, fired his gun into the air to demonstrate his gratitude.

'Supposing they all start shooting? I guess they're trigger-happy.' Mrs Schooner betrayed slight alarm through her tough veneer. 'Now we've seen a few live bandits, why bother to see the Tombs?'

The men thanked us with formal courtesy, bowing and shaking their own hands. I distributed a few coins for their journey money and we wished each other *I lu p'ing-an*, a safe and peaceful return. Our driver slunk back rather crestfallen as soon as they were out of sight. 'You were in luck. They could have shot you,' he said. 'And I could have shot them,' said Mrs Schooner, producing a pocket pistol from her leather bag.

Having come so far with that definite intention, I was anxious not to miss the Triumphal Way leading to the Tombs, but Mrs Schooner had had enough. 'I'm disappointed in the bandits,' she declared. Already she was bored and grumpy. Her subconscious had yearned for a shindy, a little bloodshed. I left her with the driver to finish the wine and relax while I wandered towards the avenue of statues in the distance. Very strange they looked, standing in couples on that desolate plain. Sculptured lions, horses, camels, griffins, unicorns, elephants, civil and military officials over life-size carved from single blocks of stone, the elephants thirteen feet high and fourteen feet long, formed a perpetual guard of honour for the funeral procession of dead emperors.

'You really ought to see the statues,' I urged Mrs Schooner. 'They are quite extraordinary if not unique. Do let me take you there.'

'Nuts to statues. I've a cocktail engagement at the embassy and my thermos flask is empty.'

The actual Tombs were ahead of us and I was sorry not to visit that of Yung Lo, the founder of modern Peking. But Mrs Schooner was stubbornly deaf to persuasion. On the way back she was silent and comatose, to my intense relief. Perhaps I was not the right companion for such a picnic. Later I heard that she had spread a romantic report of our carousal with wild bandits armed to the teeth. The remaining bottles of Pouilly were sent to my house with a note of farewell on pink writing paper with a silver monogram: 'When you come to Magnolia, Mass., I'll give you a proper picnic. Wombs not tombs, and barbecues on the beach. Aloha, as they say in Hawaii, Sincerely, Arabella Schooner.'

Harold Acton

An Indoor American Picnic

MISSY ALLEN

An indoor picnic is just like any other picnic, except that it is indoors. Indoor picnics are ideal for urban dwellers who just can't get away, or for the disappointed whose outing has to be cancelled because of bad weather. The best setting for an indoor picnic is in front of the fireplace, where you get the feeling and smell of the outdoors and the chance to 'roast' something over the 'open fire'.

You must at all times pretend that you are on a real picnic. Once the basket leaves the kitchen there can be no return trips for forgotten items (inevitable on any picnic). Even though you may be in the next room you cannot go back and will have to work with what is in the basket or available in the room in which the picnic is being held. If you forget the tin opener you'll just have to make do with the poker from the fireplace.

To enhance the pretence of an outdoor picnic and perhaps make the best of an otherwise gloomy day you should dress for the part in sundresses, shorts, floppy hats and sunglasses. If you put some strong-smelling coconut tanning lotion on the tip of your nose and sit close to the fire with your eyes closed you can pretend that you are on the beach.

Inasmuch as you won't have very far to travel you can bring along items that are often left behind on picnics. Personally I stick to paper plates and plastic glasses. First, I think they add to a picnic feeling, and secondly I don't want to wash dishes after any type of picnic.

I recommend cold chicken, potato salad, coleslaw, and hard rolls with a variety of sliced meats and cheeses so that picnickers can make their own sandwiches. Don't forget a good Dijon mustard. 'Stuffers' such as potato crisps and pretzels are good as long as you remember a large tablecloth to protect the rug. If it's a really cold day you want to bring a thermos of hot soup or cocoa, but it's more likely that in front of a hot fire you will prefer gin and tonics or wine for the grown-ups and lemonade or some other soft drink for the children. For dessert bring brownies or toast goopy marshmallows that can either be eaten 'straight' or incorporated into even goopier Samoas. After the picnic you should have a nap in front of the fire before the 'journey' home. Indoor picnics are a great boost for the spirit.

Potato Salad

8 large potatoes   1 medium onion
4 eggs   Vinaigrette, made with *moutarde de l'ancienne*
4 stalks celery   and celery seeds

Boil the potatoes and the eggs. When the potatoes are soft (a fork goes in easily) take them off the heat and cool in a strainer. Peel the potatoes and eggs. Cut in large chunks and place in a large plastic bowl with an airtight lid. Chop and add the celery. Mince and add the onion. Pour the vinaigrette over and toss well.

Samoas

Ritz honey graham crackers (or digestives)
Plain or milk chocolate bars
Marshmallows

Put two biscuits on a plate with a large piece of chocolate on each. Place two marshmallows on a stick and toast them over the fire until they are super-runny. Place the marshmallows on one cracker and cover with the other, chocolate inside. The hot marshmallow melts the chocolate and you have a goopy Samoa.

Brownies

10 oz (275 g) sugar

5 oz (150 g) butter

2 eggs

1 teaspoon vanilla essence

Pinch of salt

2 oz (50 g) plain flour

3 teaspoons cocoa
  powder

Preheat the oven to gas mark 5 (375°F, 190°C). Cream the butter and sugar, beat the eggs and add them gradually, beating after each addition. Add the vanilla. Mix the dry ingredients and fold in slowly. Place in a greased Swiss roll tin and bake for about 20 minutes.

Missy Allen-Peissel

A Breakfast Picnic

TESSA BARING

The breakfast picnic is a tradition in my husband's family, a strange race of early risers. I recommend it particularly to people with the kind of small children who wake up at five o'clock on summer mornings and are horribly bored for hours before the day is allowed to begin.

Decide on a morning which is likely to be fine, and choose a place that is remote and beautiful but not too far off a road. These picnics are most fun if shared with friends, or with cousins as we used to. Each family should bring some of the food items, and for some reason it is particularly successful if the age-range spans three generations. There is a feeling of excitement and exclusiveness at being the only people about so early in the morning, and someone is sure to remark that it is the most beautiful part of the day, and that other people are very stupid to miss it.

When you arrive at your chosen site, the first task is for children to find suitable sticks to light the camp fire, and it adds to the sense of adventure if some 'wild' food is found, such as wild raspberries or, later in the year, mushrooms. My mother-in-law has memories of breakfast picnics as a child, where the speciality was an omelette made from blackbird's eggs stolen from the nest and cooked in a doll's frying pan. (There was more countryside to go round in those days and such a thing would not have been frowned upon as it would today.) Otherwise the ingredients are those of a normal old-fashioned English breakfast: bacon, fried-eggs, fried bread (preferably brown and home-made), sausages and fried tomatoes, which are essential as they freshen up the otherwise rather greasy taste. Potato cakes also go down well early in the morning; they can be prepared in advance and brought in aluminium foil ready for frying.

It is important for someone to bring a frying pan, matches, newspaper, some form of cooking fat or oil, thermos flasks of coffee and orange juice for the children, plates, knives and forks and a few rugs, as the grass will be wet with dew. Also an oven cloth is highly recommended, and something to deal with the inevitable burnt fingers.

When the cooking has been done and you are all sitting round the fire eating the most delicious breakfast you can remember, and feeling that you are the only people in the world, it's a wonderful time for conversation.

A Scottish Recipe for Potato Cakes

2 lb (900 g) potatoes freshly boiled in their jackets
8 oz (225 g) self-raising flour
Salt

Sieve the potatoes on to a floured board, add the salt, and work in the flour by degrees, kneading lightly. Then roll out thinly, cut into rounds the size of a dinner plate, and cut each round into quarters. Fry.

Tessa Baring.

Carey's Cold Collation

CAREY BASSET

No doubt you will think that this is an appallingly badly planned menu, and you would be right; however, try it for easiness's sake and a saving on the electricity bill. And try to arrange the picnic near somebody else's fruit orchard or garden, so that guests who are sober enough to walk can pick their own pudding.

The day of my trial picnic coincided with a plague of a million tiny thunderflies; however, I pretended I had had an accident with the black pepper while making the mayonnaise, so nobody was any the wiser.

The menu is enough for four people. With the quantities given in the recipe you will get 28 small profiteroles, four savoury and three sweet for each person. The profiteroles go soft the day after they are made, so crisp them up in a very hot oven for 4 or 5 minutes. They are best eaten fresh. Taking paper plates and cups saves washing up; knives and forks aren't needed, but paper napkins are essential as one's fingers smell awful after peeling prawns.

PS. Don't forget to take water for the dogs.

Picnic Poofs

7½ fl. oz (220 ml) water
3 oz (75 g) butter
3½ oz (85 g) plain flour
3 eggs
Baking sheets

Preheat the oven to gas mark 7 (425°F, 220°C). Put the water and butter into a fairly large saucepan. Sift the flour. Bring the pan to the boil and when bubbling draw aside. Allow the bubbles to subside, then pour in all the flour at once. Stir vigorously with a wooden spoon until the mixture comes cleanly away from the sides of the pan – this happens very quickly. Allow to cool for 5 minutes and then transfer the mixture to a Magimix bowl with the double-bladed steel knife already in position. Switch on the machine and add the eggs one by one, processing after each addition until the mixture is smooth. If you don't own a Magimix you will have to beat by hand, but I must admit I've never tried it the hard way. Grease the baking sheet or sheets and hold under the cold tap; shake off surplus water. Place teaspoons of the mixture on the sheets, leaving room for expansion, and bake for about 20 minutes. If you have an Aga, as I do, place the sheets first in the baking oven, and finish in the roasting oven for the same times as given above. When baked, put on a wire rack to cool and pierce the sides with a skewer to let the steam escape, otherwise the profiteroles will be soggy inside.

Some Savoury Fillings

Scrambled egg with smoked salmon or anchovy pieces
Prawns or shrimps in mayonnaise
Lobster or crab in mayonnaise
Minced beef or other minced meats, and onion
Diced raw vegetables in mayonnaise
Cream cheese on lettuce leaves
Ham, mustard and parsley
Diced bacon and tomatoes
Caviar and sour cream

It's best to let people assemble their own fillings and not risk soggy profiteroles. However, the chocolate ones travel well.

Chocolate Poofs

4 oz (110 g) bar plain chocolate
Whipped cream

Melt the chocolate with a little water or liquid coffee in a double boiler or a basin placed over hot (not boiling) water. Split the profiteroles and fill with whipped cream. Spoon the chocolate over the tops.

Carey Bassed.

Glory's Picnic

CLEMENTINE BEIT

Our Ridgeback dog, Glory, loved picnics. He always seemed to know when one was being planned and would get into the car when he saw that it was about to be loaded up; everything was then packed around him and we would set off. On arrival at the picnic spot, he would sit and watch the baskets being unpacked, drooling with anticipation. We always took his dinner with us, and when he had wolfed it down he would do the rounds, pleading with everyone that he was still starving. There were never any scraps left to tidy away before leaving if Glory had been on a picnic!

Glory's Picnic Pudding

Spread 3 or 4 slices of bread – preferably brown – with dripping or butter, including the brown jelly from your dripping bowl if possible. Chop up some scraps and leftovers, mince (raw or cooked), and a little chopped or grated cheese (if liked by dog). Chicken skin was much liked. Cut the slices of bread into fairly small squares. Put alternative layers of bread and scraps into the dog's bowl, moisten with warm gravy or Oxo and mix up lightly with a fork – the mixture should not be too soggy. Cover the bowl with foil.

In Africa we always took water for Glory.

Clementine Beit

A Picnic for the Air

ARABELLA BOXER

In the early days of travel, passengers invariably took their food with them. Towards the end of her life, my Scottish grandmother admitted that she had never eaten a meal in public; perhaps she didn't eat when travelling, or perhaps she just didn't travel. For us, living as we did in the north of Scotland, overnight train trips were a part of life; travelling back and forth to school, visits to the dentist and optician – all involved lengthy journeys. One of the nicest things about them was sitting on the top bunk of a third-class sleeper – only our parents travelled first-class – unwrapping the greaseproof paper package of food that was meant to sustain one through the night. Torn between greed and potential travel sickness, I always ended up eating everything, but have felt unable to face the same foods since; sandwiches made with roast beef or chicken still make me feel slightly faint.

On the Trans-Siberian Express, travellers took their own uncooked food with them; the train had a special 'cold' carriage for storing semi-frozen food. Passengers would take with them a large bag of *pelmeni*, a sort of Russian ravioli, and at each station a large pot of water was kept boiling over a brazier, so that the *pelmeni* could be cooked while the train stopped. In England we were not so lucky, and all food had to be prepared in advance and packed.

Few people take packed meals on trains any more, although it would be sensible to do so. There is something slightly daunting about eating alone, surrounded by strangers who are not eating, and trips to the dining car – if there is such a thing – are fun, though expensive and gastronomically disappointing. If, however, one is travelling by air, there is a very strong case for taking one's own food, and one's own drink as well. In the early days of Laker flights this was essential, for food was not provided, and it seemed an eminently sensible economy. From the passenger's point of view, taking one's own food on any regular airline is not of course an economy, since meals are provided free, but rather a sensible form of insurance. This is especially true, paradoxically, when travelling first-class, for the food and drink that are then pressed on us are even less suited to our needs than the ordinary fare. In fact, I have recently discovered that most airlines will provide special vegetarian meals if they are ordered a day or two in advance. Being lower in protein, and more easily digested, they provide a reasonable alternative for occasions when preparing a 'home-cooked' meal is impractical.

When flying, our system is under strain from a number of different factors. The most obvious one is pressure: although the aircraft is pressurized, for technical reasons it cannot be brought down to the pressure that most of us are accustomed to – sea level. Instead, it is kept at the pressure found between six and seven thousand feet – within moments of entering the plane our bodies have to adjust to a significant change in environment. Pressurization causes the gases in our system to dilate, creating an unpleasant feeling of distention. For this reason it is important not to drink fizzy liquids.

The second main reason for feeling less than well is the dehydration of the air in the cabin. This puts the kidneys under strain since it is their job to regulate the balance of water in the blood. When we are in danger of becoming dehydrated, the pituitary gland produces large amounts of anti-diuretic hormone, causing the kidneys to re-absorb into the bloodstream much of the water which would have been excreted. In order to offset this dehydration, it is vital to drink a great deal; for short journeys, roughly one pint for every hour spent in the air is advisable, while for long trips a quarter of a pint per hour is more realistic. Still mineral water or hot herb teas are ideal.

Alcohol should be avoided at all costs. First it exacerbates dehydration, and secondly it causes extra work for the liver which is already operating under strain. The liver is responsible for breaking down and getting rid of poisons absorbed into the body, for example those contained in alcohol, caffeine and nicotine. When travelling, the liver is already under pressure and less able than usual to cope with these tasks, so that drinking alcohol and coffee and smoking should be avoided. Smoking in particular makes people feel unwell, since the degree of carbon monoxide in the body is increased by the thin air circulating in the cabin, so that normal conditions are exaggerated. The liver also controls the degree of acidity in the body, so that very acid foods such as citrus fruits should be kept to a minimum. Champagne is a good example of what to avoid, since it combines three of the worst things: alcohol, acidity and gas.

In addition to the strains caused by pressurization, dehydration, altitude and speed other stresses are normally connected with travel: fatigue, anxiety and, in many cases, fear of flying itself. All these affect the nervous system, which in turn affects the digestion, therefore foods that put an undue strain on the digestive organs should be avoided. Rich foods, due to their high fat content, come into this category, as do foods that are high in protein. Meat, eggs and cheese should only be eaten in very small quantities, while indigestible foods like hard-boiled eggs and cold potatoes (i.e. potato salad) are also best left out. Highly spiced food like salami is also unsuitable, while garlic is clearly anti-social, to say the least.

A good general rule is to drink as much as possible, remembering to stick to still, non-alcoholic drinks, and to eat as little as possible. The food should be similar to that given to a convalescent: bland, light, easy to digest and appetizing. It should be moderate in temperature, neither iced nor boiling hot. Creamy vegetable soups, so long as they are not too rich, salads, small pieces of chicken or white fish, cooked vegetables, (except potatoes), rice, fruit, yoghurt and low-fat cream cheese are all good. Still mineral water should be carried in generous quantities; it is no good relying on the stewardess to bring you water, for she will be too busy, and the glasses are minute. Mineral water, especially a still one, is rarely among the drinks on offer. (A 'bottle' bag for carrying a large bottle of mineral water can always be used later to carry off duty-free drink bought on the plane.) Tea bags of herb tea are useful, since these are easily diluted with hot water when the stewardess does the coffee.

Planning a picnic to take from home is relatively simple, but finding a suitable meal to bring back, without a base to prepare it, is another matter. Yet most other countries are better equipped for this sort of thing than we are, and a brief visit to a delicatessen just before leaving will usually provide mineral water, vegetable juice (for a soup substitute), bread, butter, fruit, yoghurt and a low-fat cheese such as fromage blanc or ricotta.

It is both sensible and fun to shop around to build up a small picnic kit. A light basket with a lid, or a small cool-bag, equipped with plastic plate and beaker, two plastic containers with lids, plus knife, fork and spoon, should cover every eventuality. Those who abhor plastic can find old horn beakers, reminiscent of shooting parties, in antique shops, while a wooden plate can replace the plastic one, although it will be heavier. Once the habit has become established, it takes little time to prepare a couple of simple dishes before leaving, and the benefit in avoiding, or at least decreasing, the after-effects of air travel will certainly repay the extra effort.

Menus for Air Picnics

1. Creamy leek soup
   Potted shrimps
   Brown bread and butter sandwich
   Yoghurt

2. Cold cucumber soup with dill
   Breast of poached chicken wrapped in a lettuce leaf
   Watercress salad
   Crême caramel, baked in an *oeuf en cocotte* dish

3. Prawn and crisp lettuce salad
   Sandwich of brown bread and butter and cress, or watercress
   Petits Suisses

4. Beef tea
   Chicken salad
   Matzos or Ryvita
   Grated apple in yoghurt

5. Chicken broth (in thermos)
   Salad of cooked vegetables
   Plums, grapes or cherries

6. Flaked white fish in mayonnaise-type dressing
   Watercress salad
   Brown bread and butter
   Low-fat cream cheese

7. Creamy potato and chervil soup (cold)
   Spinach and mozzarella salad
   Apricots with yoghurt

To drink: Volvic or other still mineral water
Peppermint, verbena or sage tea

Arabella Boxer.

Gaveston Picnic, 1981

JONATHAN BURNHAM

The self-styled *beau monde* of Oxford undergraduate life is headed by a collection of dining clubs which are, for the most part, defiantly all-male. Their style varies from the solemn and stuffy to the racy and frivolous, the Piers Gaveston Society falling very much into the latter category. The club was originally based within Oriel, a college founded by Gaveston's close friend Edward II, and its aims are to pay a back-handed tribute to Gaveston's amorality, and so to set a tone of wickedness lacking in other exclusively male gatherings. Thus for the club to hold a summer picnic on the banks of the Isis was the fitting counterpart to, say, the Bullingdon's decorous white-tie dinner the same week.

In the event the picnic gained spice from the nearness of finals and the presence of a wide-eyed bunch of new junior members – known as minions – who feared the worst. The thirteen members met at a riverside pub, dressed in cricket whites and club tie, and decamped to a secluded part of the river bank, where the local Oxford photographer set up his tripod and took the annual club picture.

Although girlfriends, stoically resigned to their exclusion, had thoughtfully offered to prepare elaborate pâtés and the like, it was decided that a simple meal of Parma ham, melon, Brie, french bread, peaches and hock had the right note of masculine unfussiness along with luxury. Before the meal minutes were taken by the 'Keeper of the Annals', who recorded the only absence as being that of the club's President, 'The Poker', who had decided to go off to Wimbledon for the day. It was thus for the second-in-command, the Master of Debaucheries, to take charge, and he promptly proposed that all minions (the butt of all forfeits) should pretend they were the artist's models in *Déjeuner sur l'herbe*. The Dispenser (re-named Di-Spenser that summer of the royal wedding) then sconced the Master for 'lasciviousness', and was sconced himself for finding lasciviousness a sconce-able offence and thereby going against club policy.

During the meal the usual gallivanting exhibited by the club during its celebrations rather lost its point in the absence of spectators, apart from a tranquil herd of cows on the opposite bank which was treated to a display of antics with *baguettes* and club ties. A grim-looking rowing team from the Dragon School slogged past and was pelted with the over-ripe peaches. The Master called a stop to the schoolboyishness of it all, and asked for a serious discussion of the dress for that term's fancy-dress ball. The idea being to choose a theme that suited the Gaveston ethic, suggestions poured out – 'Imperial Leather', 'Able Seamen', 'Roman Camp', 'Our Future Queen', and 'Going Down', of which the last was considered to have the most connotations. After that two minions decided to inaugurate popular games – an inspired idea, since there was unlimited space and the right spirit of theatricality present, combined with the effects of the wine. The picnic stretched into the late afternoon, and broke up only as the hock became warm and unpalatable, and older members recalled the following days' exams.

Jonathan Burnham.

A Country Churchyard Picnic

JOHN CHANCELLOR

It might be thought that a churchyard is a macabre venue for a picnic. Picnics are, after all, supposed to be cheerful occasions, when you are not expected to entertain thoughts of death. The most fearless and unimaginative of us might hesitate before spreading the contents of a picnic basket upon a tombstone. Who knows how its ghostly occupant would take it?

Some churchyards are more inviting than others. An example of a friendly churchyard is that in the village of Selborne in Hampshire, the home of the immortal Gilbert White. It is universally agreed that Gilbert White has given delight to generations; but who he was and the exact nature of this 'delight' is known to very few. Nevertheless the book, upon which rests his unshakeable yet elusive fame, has been reprinted almost every year since it was published in 1789, with the title *The Natural History and Antiquities of Selborne*.

The opportunity offered itself one Sunday in September to make an expedition to Selborne. My son was at school at Winchester, where once or twice a term I took him out. These occasions were pleasant enough, but shockingly expensive. I learned there that it was not only in London that the price of a meal in a restaurant was scandalous. Admittedly, he did not make a point of going for the cheaper items, and I was amazed at the number of gin and tonics that he managed to drink. It was my sister who, horrified at seeing me pay over a vast sum for one of these Winchester meals (two of her daughters were there also), insisted that the next time we took the boy out, it would be a picnic or nothing.

So we found ourselves on that Sunday in September making our way from Winchester to Selborne. All the members of the party were united by the haziness of their knowledge as to who or what Gilbert White was. My son, furthermore, had the temerity to doubt the extent of the delight that White had given later generations. These doubts were, alas, to intensify as the day went on.

We passed through many a charming village before reaching our destination. This was the moment to prepare my captive companions for the great experience ahead of them, to acquaint them with the 'genius' of Gilbert White. On that very week, two hundred years earlier, he had made these observations in his journal:

Black snails lie out, and copulate. Vast swagging clouds . . . red-breasts feed on elder-berries, enter rooms, and spoil the furniture . . . women make poor wages in their hop-picking. Housed all my potatoes, and tied up my endives . . . swallows hawking about very briskly in all the moderate rain . . . then we called loudly thro' the speaking trumpet to Timothy [his tortoise], he does not seem to regard the noise.

There were few swagging clouds on that particular Sunday, and we lacked the acuteness of observation to notice how many black snails were copulating.

The entries in his journal explain perhaps why Gilbert White occupies so firm a place in the heart of the normal, wholesome Englishman. The English like their heroes to be simple and unaffected, to be stay-at-home and unambitious, and to be disinterested in the activities they pursue, thinking of neither gain nor fame. Gilbert White was all these things. He spent his whole life in the same house at Selborne; he never aspired to be more than a curate, and he recorded meticulously, day after day, what he saw happening in the countryside around him. All this he had put down in *Selborne*, that little-read classic of English literature, a copy of which I had not forgotten to bring on this expedition. It was my plan to read aloud during our picnic one or two of its imperishable passages.

We entered the village, at the end of which we came to Selborne church and churchyard, described by White as 'very scanty . . . such a mass of mortality that no person can be interred there without disturbing or displacing the bones of his ancestors'. We squeezed ourselves between several tombstones, very near the splendid yew tree with an enormous girth which White measured every year in his meticulous and disinterested way. He also observed that it was a male tree.

Whilst the others tucked in, I expatiated on the greatness and modesty of Gilbert White and began to read aloud from the famous book. Maybe I chose one of the less stimulating passages – it was about the diversity of soils in the district – or maybe the solemnity of the occasion overcame them, or maybe it was my sister's delicious food, but when I looked up my companions were, one and all, dozing among the tombstones.

Cauliflower Salad

1–2 cauliflowers	1 teaspoon mixed mustard
Salt	1 oz (25 g) sugar
Pepper	1 oz (25 g) butter
Cayenne	4 tablespoons milk
2 eggs	3 tablespoons sugar

Cook the cauliflowers in boiling salted water. Don't overcook – let them retain a little 'bite'. Then leave them in a colander to drain. Divide into small florets and place in a salad bowl. Season well with pepper, salt and cayenne and make the following sauce.

Beat the eggs in a double boiler. Add a level teaspoon of salt, the mustard, sugar, butter, milk and vinegar. Stir over boiling water till it thickens. Then pour over the salad, or bottle and pour over before it is served.

Mint Lemonade

4 large lemons
1 handful fresh mint
4 bottles ginger ale
8 oz (225 g) sugar

Squeeze the lemons and strain the juice. Add the sugar and stir until dissolved. Put into a chilled thermos with mint and some ice cubes. Pack the chilled ginger ale separately in an insulated bag and add just before serving.

John Chancellor

Suprême de Volaille with St George in Cappadocia

PENELOPE CHETWODE

After an interval of thirty years, I returned to India in 1963 by the overland route. A young doctor friend bought a second-hand Volkswagen Dormobile from a farmer near Wantage and proceeded to make a green roll-up tent on his mother's sewing machine – which has never worked since. The tent, fixed to the roof of the vehicle, could be unrolled and set up as a roomy lean-to shelter within five minutes of arriving at any camp site. The cooking was done in it on two primus stoves, and there was room for three people to sleep on the ground while two of us slept in the Dormobile.

In those far-off days petrol cost the equivalent of 20p a gallon, and by the time we reached Delhi the captain (as we called the doctor) calculated he had spent about £100 on it after driving some five to six thousand miles. We took two months to complete the journey since we wanted to do as much sightseeing as possible in Turkey and Iran, and foodwise our life was one great picnic as we had all our meals *al fresco* except when we spent a few nights in great cities like Istanbul, Ankara and Teheran.

The cooking was done on the primus stoves because the captain had been informed that gas cylinders were unobtainable in many places on our route, and that wood was virtually non-existent throughout Turkey and Iran. I well remember meeting two Swiss boys who were travelling to India on a Vespa and had planned to buy food on their way and cook it on bonfires. Since there was no wood lying about in the treeless wilds of Anatolia they were almost starving – they had to fill themselves up in restaurants in the towns they came through and had hardly any money left.

Primus stoves are so fierce that the ideal pot to use on them is a pressure cooker. I used to cook our supper in one every night, so that we could usually eat within an hour of setting up camp. We eventually got rather bored with the mutton we bought in the Turkish bazaars and thought that chicken would be a welcome change. Accordingly when we came to a small town called Nevsehir, crowned by an Ottoman fortress, we tried to make some men understand that we wanted to buy poultry, but they took us to the police station! There we began to flap our arms up and down and cluck loudly, and everyone laughed and understood perfectly what we wanted. We were taken to a large farmyard on the outskirts of the town where a number of scrawny little cockerels and hens were scratching around. With the permission of the farmer (using the language of gesticulation) we caught two. Now having had a poultry farm, I had learnt the quickest and most humane way to kill chickens. I dispatched the pair by dislocating their heads from the necks, handed one to the captain and advised him to pluck it at once while I did the other, as they are so much easier to feather when they are still warm. Disgruntled murmurs immediately arose from the many onlookers who had accompanied us out of the town, and I suddenly realized the reason. I had let no blood, and Moslems as well as Jews insist on this being done, so we quickly paid for the birds, beat a hasty retreat into the Dormobile, and drove off to Urgup, some twelve miles further on, plucking as we went.

We now found ourselves in the most extraordinary landscape in the middle of Cappadocia: for about twenty miles through a valley erosion has left huge cones about a hundred feet high, some of which look like decaying teeth, others like towers, needles and pyramids formed of ashes and rock. These are collectively known as the Rock-cut Monasteries of Cappadocia because, during the seventh and eighth centuries, whole communities of Christians settled in the area and cut out of the rock churches and monasteries which they decorated with wall paintings in the provincial Byzantine style. It was very rewarding to come across many renderings of St George killing his dragon, as he is traditionally believed to have come from this part of Turkey.

We found a wonderful camp site at the head of the valley in a small sandy field with superb views and a large rock wall to one side over which we hung our bedding to dry during the day. We became so enthralled exploring the churches and monasteries and anchorites' cells that we ended up spending three nights there.

But to return to the supper picnic on the evening of our arrival. I decided to prepare a suprême de volaille by cooking the elderly, tough little chickens in the pressure cooker, and the rice in an open saucepan on the other stove. After half an hour I wanted to let the pressure down quickly so that I could get on with making the sauce out of the stock. In the centre of a pressure cooker is a weight; when you lift if off it makes a violent hissing sound which always terrifies me, so I asked the captain if he dared do it. He immediately removed not just the weight but the whole lid, whereupon the cooked birds leaped high into the air and disappeared in the inky blackness of a moonless night!

We were all mad with disappointment at being thus deprived of what had promised to be one of the most gastronomically exciting picnics of our journey, but we did not give up hope. For the next twenty minutes we all crawled about on our hands and knees and, with the aid of two very feeble torches, we finally ran them to earth – literally, for they were covered with the dusty grey soil of the region. Undaunted, we plunged them into a bucket of water and, while the girls washed and jointed them, I made a delicious sauce suprême with fat, flour, the stock, a little dried milk powder, and the juice of half a small lemon. I did not add the extra refinement of egg yolks as our egg supply was low and we needed them for breakfast.

We finally sat down in a circle round our old hurricane lamp to a scrumptious meal of chicken and rice and sauce and green beans that we had bought in the market at Nevsehir, followed by delicious little white grapes, and all washed down by unadulterated spring water. Water in Turkey is famous for its excellence and the Turks, who are forbidden wine by their religion, talk rapturously of the water of various regions as others would of the wines in France or Italy.

I think our Cappadocian chicken picnic was the best we had on the whole trip, all the more for being so hard won. I was also very proud of the jam roly-poly I made when we were allowed to camp in the harem of Xerxes in Persepolis but that, as Kipling would say, is another story.

Penelope Chetwode

Glyndebourne: A Critical View of the Picnic

GEORGE CHRISTIE

Picnics are difficult to stomach. I for one don't have much appetite for them. The human body, it seems to me, is not a suitable shape for eating in comfort at ground level. Eating in this fashion ought to be anti-digestive; and so it should follow that the second half of any performance at Glyndebourne gets a dyspeptic reception. Less than 50 per cent of the audience can be fed in the restaurant – so something over thirty thousand people picnic in the Glyndebourne gardens each year, a disturbing volume of dyspepsia in my book.

However, the British music critic confounds this theory. He is convinced that the Glyndebourne audience is recklessly receptive to the second part of a performance, having suffered or tolerated the first. Is the Glyndebourne audience a glutton for punishment, as I suspect? Or is the Glyndebourne audience simply a glutton, as the British music critic would like us to believe? Or does the British music critic himself tend to picnic at Glyndebourne and so prove the theory that cynicism is born of dyspepsia? Thirty thousand eating their way through their picnics in the relentless rain of the 1980 summer must surely have tested the audience's resilience. But their frailty remains to be proved. The box office for 1981 was as snowed under as ever. Perhaps the audience comes for the performance rather than the picnic . . .

In 1976 a device was introduced to make picnics more palatable at Glyndebourne. A large marquee was put up in the grounds, a result of the munificence of W. D. and H. O. Wills. At a ceremony held to celebrate the opening of this marquee, I made a few fatuous remarks about hoping for a wet summer. It turned out to be the hottest, driest summer in recorded history, and the marquee was a wasted asset. Everybody was praying for the rains. The next three summers answered their prayers and swamped the place – so we had to extend the marquee (and, I hope, the receptivity of the audience as well as that of the British music critic).

The picnic ritual at Glyndebourne is relentlessly publicized. Many of the foreign critics devote the first part of their 'appreciation' to a description of the resemblance of the Friesian cattle on one side of the ha-ha to the audience grazing on the other. They invariably devote the next part of their 'appreciation' to a nostalgic, rather than pertinent, walk down Glyndebourne's memory lane; and as a token to their profession as critics, they throw in at the end a line or two about the performance which straddles either side of the picnic.

One of the little foibles of Glyndebourne's picnickers is to tie bits of string round the neck of their bottles and moor them to the banks of the ponds to keep the wine cool. One audience member fell in while dragging his bottle out. A resourceful usher showed the luckless man to the wardrobe department, who helped him out with a smart costume from the Bal Blanc scene from the final act of *Eugene Onegin*. The man enjoyed his Blanc de Blanc and turned out to be a critic from California. The enthusiasm of his article was effusive. The temptation to encourage critics to moor their bottles is a strong one, but I suppose it must be resisted!

George Christie.

A Picnic in Portugal

COLETTE CLARK

The best food I have eaten on a picnic was cooked by a farmer's wife in a tiny village in northern Portugal. My brother had asked her for something to take with us on a walk up the foothills of the Minho mountains in search of a series of waterfalls, and this is what she provided: two freshly cooked marinated chickens from her own farmyard; slices of cold veal coated in a spicy glacé sauce; meat and egg croquettes (*croquetas*) which were still warm but of such perfect consistency – firm but light – that they could be eaten with the fingers. To this were added home-made bread rolls, tomatoes and fruit from her garden and, to crown it all, little cold pancakes filled with cherry jam and dusted with cinnamon. But it is the croquettes I will remember.

Egg Croquettes

1½ oz (40 g) butter	4 hard-boiled eggs
1½ oz flour (40 g) flour	2 raw egg yolks
8 fl. oz (200 ml) milk	Parsley
flavoured with salt,	Salt
pepper and bayleaf	Fresh white breadcrumbs
Pinch of nutmeg	Oil and butter for frying

Make a sauce by melting the butter, adding the flour, and cooking to make the roux. Add the milk gradually, stirring all the time. Cook for 5 minutes, then leave to cool a little. Add the chopped eggs, one egg yolk, parsley and nutmeg. Leave on a plate to get cold (it is best to prepare up to this point the night before, or several hours in advance if that is not possible).

Roll into fat sausage shapes on a board covered in seasoned flour, then dip into the beaten yolk of an egg to which you have also added salt. Then roll in a large quantity of fresh white crumbs and fry in a mixture of very hot oil and butter until golden brown (a basket which can be lowered into the fat makes this easier). Drain on kitchen paper one by one, and leave to cool for the picnic.

Meat Croquettes

12 oz (350 g) cooked veal or beef	½ pint (250 ml) good gravy
1 onion	Parsley
½ oz (10 g) butter	1 beaten egg
	Breadcrumbs

Mince the meat in a Magimix for just a second or two. Chop the onion and soften in the butter in a frying pan. Add the meat, parsley, gravy, salt and pepper. The consistency should be moist, but firm enough to shape into croquettes once it has cooled down. Then proceed as for egg croquettes.

Colette Clark

A Picnic by the Fountain of Perseus and Andromeda, Holkham, Norfolk

VALERIA COKE

We usually take our picnics to the beach, a mile away, but on one hot sunny day that I remember we moved only as far as the fountain. When it plays, the fountain is spectacular; but we turn it on only when the house is open to the public as it works on a very complicated system. A vast amount of water is pumped up seven hundred feet from a well – said to be the deepest in Norfolk – to a reservoir a mile up the hill. The pressure of water from this reservoir is so great that, when the taps are turned on, it provides a magnificent display.

On the occasion that I am recalling it was a perfect summer afternoon, and before lunch the braver children clambered down the steps into the pool to swim and play hide-and-seek behind the spouting dolphins. Our picnic consisted of sorrel soup, local Cromer crab pâté, a simple quiche decorated with samphire from the marsh, and an equally simple but delicious pudding.

Sorrel Soup

8 oz (225 g) mixed sorrel
  and lettuce
2 oz (50 g) butter
1 pint (500 ml)
  chicken stock

2 egg yolks
½ pint (250 ml) cream
Salt
Black pepper
Grated nutmeg

Wash and dry the leaves, removing the stalks. Heat the butter in a heavy pan, add the sorrel and lettuce and cook gently for 3 minutes. Heat the stock and pour on. Bring to simmering point, add a little salt and cover the pan. Simmer for 5 minutes. Put in a liquidizer or through a mouli. Beat the egg yolks with the cream, stir in one ladleful of hot soup and return to the mixture. Add the black pepper and nutmeg to taste. Reheat but do not boil. Serve hot or cold.

Crab Pâté

1 lb (450 g) crab meat	1 clove garlic, crushed
2–3 tablespoons mayonnaise	Cayenne
1 dessertspoon curry powder	Melted butter

Add the garlic, curry powder and cayenne to the mayonnaise, and mix with the crab meat to a firm consistency. Press down in an earthenware pot or soufflé dish. Pour on melted butter to seal. Serve with toast or fresh bread and salad.

Raspberries and White Currants in Soured Cream

Mix raspberries and topped and tailed white currants together, dredge with caster sugar, and lightly fold in soured cream.

Picnic at the Grange

NICHOLAS COLERIDGE

I don't know of a more perfect setting for a picnic than the ruins of Grange Park. This is the astonishing Greek Revival house near Micheldever in Hampshire that C. R. Cockerell built for the Baring family, and around which there was so much controversy a few years ago when plans were made to knock it down. Now the shell of the house stands, like the ruins of Priene, at the head of a valley surrounded by cornfields with distant views of a lake beyond.

It is such a dramatic setting that any picnic staged there is a colossal leap upmarket. Even half-a-dozen bread rolls and a slice of veal and ham pie looks rather good eaten underneath the portico of the ballroom, which is the best place to set up a picnic table. All around the ruin are clumps of nettles and dock leaves which conceal quite large fragments of frieze and, if you are very lucky, pieces of broken sculpture. It is rather like scavenging over the plains of Troy except that no little boys rush up with faked antiquities for sale. Until recently you could have vandalized the Neo-Classical mantelpieces too, some of which were suspended in mid-air between floorless rooms. We talked about it a lot, but you would have needed a crane. Last time I went, however, they had all disappeared and there were deep gaping holes in the plaster. We presumed that a Fulham antique dealer had made a hit-and-run assault with a van at dead of night.

The only disadvantage of Grange Park is that it is impossible to find. I have picnicked there several times and on each occasion driven for hours in convoy, up and down hill, endlessly three-point-turning, pulling into lay-bys at every summit and agreeing that we *must* be able to see it from here. The lanes around Micheldever all look exactly the same and only every half hour or so, when you pass the railway station for the third time, do you realize that you've been driving in a circle.

The entrance to the house is guarded by a lodge and this you must drive past at great speed. Once past, however, there is little chance of being nabbed for trespassing. Grange Park is now run by the Department of the Environment, who have surrounded it with barbed wire and 'Clear off' type signs but haven't, so far, installed a watchman.

My first Grange Park outing was with friends then at the Courtauld Institute of Art, plus Napier Miles who claims to know that part of Hampshire inside out and was map reading, but really only knows it back to front. Our intended lunch had turned into picnic tea by the time we found the house and suddenly it had become very cold. All I can remember is everybody huddled in tartan car rugs sitting on the roof. Possibly we were singing old pop songs to keep warm (I do hope that we weren't). Then someone suggested having a discotheque, with music from the cassette player in the car. This was driven across the bumpy ground to the front of the ballroom portico, and looked like a Ford Fiesta in a colour magazine advertisement. We bopped ludicrously away to David Bowie and Dolly Parton, the music blaring through the open car door. Only when it was time to go home, however, did we realize the snag. The car battery had gone flat and we had to push.

My other notable picnic there was on the hottest Bank Holiday Monday of 1980. We had only taken an hour to find the gate this time, and two even more idiosyncratic carloads were in convoy.

In the sun Grange Park looks like the Acropolis, despite the scaffolding that the Department of the Environment have put around the ballroom to make it resemble the Pompidou Centre in Paris. We were better prepared this time, with a wind-up gramophone and a far superior picnic. Also more to drink.

Could the drink have been the spur for the preposterous photocall after lunch? This was a quite unforeseen craze for recreating old master paintings for the camera. Draped in the tablecloth and lengths of barbed wire, we cut a swathe through the Renaissance to the Pre-Raphaelites in half a dozen well-chosen frames: Guido Reni's *Ecce Homo*; Poussin's *Christ Expelling the Money-lenders from the*

Temple; the *Laocoon*; Burne-Jones's *Virgil and Dante Meeting at the River Styx*.

That is the secret ingredient in a Grange Park picnic – the culture factor. If you know anything at all, however banal, about art or architecture you can depend on an opportunity to show off. Certainly it is the only occasion ever that I can consciously recall utilizing my end-of-bin Cambridge history of art degree.

Nicholas Coleridge

Holkham Beach Picnic

SILVIA COMBE

During the summer holidays of the 1920s when, in retrospect, every day was fine, the Holkham nursery party followed an unvarying routine. Punctually at 2.30 the horse-drawn wagonette, driven by Mr Everett, the second coachman, drew up at the porter's lodge. In it embarked children, dogs, nannies, nurserymaids and picnic baskets. The drive to the sea went through Holkham village, Lady Anne's drive, and then left in the pinewoods to the Meal House, passing through blackberry bushes en route. The horse was taken out of the shafts. Everyone disembarked and the trek over the sandhills to the beach began – a superb beach with miles of sand unsullied by humans, and the sea far off in the distance. All the children insisted on bathing in the North Sea whatever the weather, the icy wind often whipping up the sand to sting their bare legs, but the verdict always was that the water was 'boiling'. After that, and the long trek to the sea and back, came a marvellous tea with masses of jam sandwiches, ginger biscuits, plum cake, and milk or tea according to one's age – followed by an exciting game of cops and robbers in the sandhills. At six the wagonette was ready to take us all home, when we were put to bed tired and happy after another glorious Holkham Beach day.

Melting Moments

2½ oz (60 g) lard
6 oz (175 g) self-raising flour
1½ oz (40 g) margarine
½ egg

3 oz (75 g) caster sugar
1 tablespoon vanilla essence
Porridge oats
Glacé cherries to decorate

Preheat the oven to gas mark 4 (350° F, 180° C). Cream the fat and sugar and beat in the beaten egg. Fold in the flour and vanilla essence. Roll into balls with wet hands, then coat with oats. Place on a greased tray and press out slightly. Bake for 15–20 minutes. Place a cherry on top of each cake.

Sponge Cake

3 eggs
4 oz (110 g) sugar
3 oz (75 g) self-raising flour
1 tablespoon hot water

Preheat the oven to gas mark 7 (425° F, 220° C). Whisk the eggs and sugar until creamy. Fold in the flour and add the water. Reduce heat to gas mark 5 (375° F, 190° C). Bake in two greased 7-inch tins for 15 minutes. Turn out and cool on a wire tray. This sponge always turns out light and delicious, and can be filled with jam, butter cream or fresh fruit. It must be eaten the same day, because its lack of fat means it will not keep.

Caramel Shortbread

2 oz (50 g) margarine
2 oz (50 g) sugar
7 oz (200 g) self-raising flour

Topping

4 oz (110 g) margarine
2 tablespoons golden syrup
4 oz (110 g) caster sugar

1 small tin condensed
  milk
8 oz (225 g) chocolate

Preheat the oven to gas mark 7 (425° F, 220° C). Cream the margarine and the sugar and fold in the flour. Press into a large greased Swiss roll tin and bake for 5 minutes.

To make the topping melt all the ingredients except the chocolate together in a pan, stirring for 5 minutes until creamy. Spread the mixture onto the shortbread and, when cool, cover with the chocolate melted in a cup over hot (not boiling) water.

This shortbread is wonderful and much appreciated by all ages.

Silvia Coombe

Picnic with the Poles, 1941

SILVIA COMBE

In the hot summer of 1941 many Polish soldiers found themselves in Angus, Scotland, after the fall of France. Members of the Tenth Mounted Rifle Regiment, they were very brave and gallant, good company and excellent dancers. They had a great success with the local females, though perhaps were not so popular with the males! There was Bridget's Pole, Sophie's Pole, Peggy's Pole, etc., etc. Communication was carried on in indifferent but voluble French, and a good time was had by all.

Some of the officers used to come for evening picnics held on the edge of Lintrathan Loch, a lovely lake surrounded by pine woods with distant views of the Grampian Hills. Food was scarce in those days of rationing, and quite often the picnic was delayed until the hens had laid enough eggs. Luckily the Poles were well laden with booze, which they drank in incredible mixtures – whisky, gin and sherry all together – but they had very strong heads and were never the worse for wear. After one merry evening by the loch one of the most attractive of the officers, called Richard, plunged in for a refreshing swim. He had not realized that he was swimming in the Dundee water supply reservoir, and was chased by two irate Water Board officials in a boat – and that, sadly, was the last of the Polish picnics by the lake.

Baked Omelette

Beaten eggs	Finely chopped onion
Seasoning	Finely chopped bacon
Chopped herbs	or chicken

Preheat the oven to gas mark 7 (425° F, 220° C). Mix all the ingredients together. Bake in buttered shallow containers (I use small enamel plates) as many very thin individual omelettes as required. Fold in half when cold. Freshly potted shrimps or asparagus tips may be added before folding.

Silvia Combe

Memories of Chantilly

DIANA COOPER

I have loved picnics for more than eighty years, ever since a feeder embroidered 'Don't be dainty' in cross-stitch was tied around my baby neck – and still do, when I am supported by strong hands to the site, and watch the baskets opened and the unexpected unwrapped. Where once it was hard-boiled egg, dry, curly meat sandwiches and perhaps a banana, eaten anywhere, it is now deliberately a surprise of rareness – iced phantasies, cups of fresh fruits, nameless delicacies, gobbled or sipped in selected venues of sunlight or speckled shade and shine . . . by the water, on the hilltop, darkly in a tropic wood, or warmed on a rug with mulled wine and ginger against the dangerous beauty of blanketing snow.

In arranging picnics I regard the element of surprise almost as an essential. Classical busts of emperors, in a very wide circle – in the heart of a forest in France, where I once lived – all had to be dressed and elaborately hatted, for instance, and I must be the most astonished of the guests. Surprise forbids attendants, anticipation and talk to announce the diversion. Once, towards the middle of a summer's evening, with the customary seven or eight friends munching their chicken, that particular picnic's perpetrator said, 'Listen, you've got to be good about this! No, no, you *must* – my neighbour, Madame de X, a sad widow with a very sick son, begged me to cheer her up by bringing you round for coffee and dessert. I knew you'd all be odious about it – but it's ten minutes away and we'll be back within the hour. Please help! No, I can't go alone.'

They followed in fury and found themselves in the early night on an eighteenth-century stone terrace with ice creams, liqueurs – no widow – a couple of young lovers and a half moon. Their relief brought the picnic its high spirits – so there we laughed and sang, out of tune, for two hours.

I think my highwater mark of surprise picnics was one that took place countless years ago, when I was living at Chantilly. Cruising around, I discovered a lake surrounded with statues and a sensible, beautiful boathouse. The nobleman who owned it – unknown to me – on solicitation allowed me a picnic on a Sunday. A few guests were staying at my little château in the Chantilly Park. My four or five weekenders and one millionaire from Paris, all expecting a none-too-good lunch at 1.30, were told that we must see this lovely lake at 12.30 – well worth a slight delay. Sudden panic! A message from an 'agent' told me that M. le Comte would be shooting that morning, but should be shot out by 12.30.

So off we all went at 12.40 through a forest where stood some kind of post round which were laid aperitifs (strong) and usual and unusual scraps. 'Good God!' I cried, 'Look what the Count has left us! What courtesy!' Beneath the speckling sun we quaffed and nibbled and blessed nobility.

This little delight was not two hundred yards from the marvellous lake, and one impatient guest sneaked off for a preview. She returned, panting, having recognized my china and pictures, to tell us with a wink from me that she had seen a lunch for eight in the boathouse, with flowers and fruit and bottles – a surprise indeed! And there we feasted, before my total exhaustion.

I have witnessed and delighted in official picnics – and one especially I can never forget, though it was the opposite of surprise. It was with Winston Churchill, no less, in Marrakesh in 1944. The site was chosen with meticulous care, on the brink of a baby canyon chosen at African dawn after two hours' search by Lady Churchill and a daughter and me – a dramatic scenario with a steep footpath through rocks and hazards of all kinds.

The 'start' was at midday and consisted of quite a procession – a food waggon, two or three chairs, linen, rugs, and implements of all sorts in another van, which included a sprinkling of police and detectives. These were followed by four or five picnickers' cars, including (to enliven my heart) Lord Beaverbrook – beloved assistant of the Prime Minister's court; and quite a few young people like flowers, gathered from I knew not where. On arrival at one o'clock the tables were laid, the rugs spread and chairs arranged – I think for the PM, Lord Beaverbrook, and Lord Moran, the great doctor, always in devoted yet mute attendance.

During this planning the young and middle-aged (myself included) took a spirited rash dash down the craggy path to look nearer the rapid, foaming little river and its huge boulders. The young men were soon half-nude and splashing hardily and scrambling none too nimbly over massive rocks. Proudly we swarmed up that fearful path again to a welcome of drinks and appreciation of our description of the dangers we had passed.

The meal, as always, because of its rarity and difference, passed hilariously, with plenty of elderly wit and youthful zest, ending with coffee, dates and brandy galore. 'Lord Moran thinks I should have another glass of brandy.' Several times Lord Moran's unspoken orders were obeyed and I realized suddenly what was inevitable – namely Winston's resolve to go down the canyon's perilous path. No word of protest either from Lord Moran or from the great man's wife! The young were not perturbed. I was properly alarmed and stood breathless with the elders halfway down to watch, thank God, his safe descent, supported by police and detectives.

At the bottom, where the young and tipsy started trying to scale again with greater enthusiasm these smooth boulders, Winston Churchill must try too, and, what's more, with the dragging and pushing of strong detectives, he succeeded in sprawling successfully to the top of them. Watching, I could think only of his steep return, of his fatigue, of his dear heart. I thought of his being dragged up by his arms so soon after lunch. 'A rope, a rope!' If only I could get one round the Prime Minister's middle so he could be pulled up smoothly. No good, no rope. All I could find was a very long and narrow white tablecloth. It would have to do. I seized it and tore down the perilous path. Anxiety shod my feet with sureness, and success crowned the effort. The dear man revelled in the relief of laying his weight upon the offered support, and reached the top daisy-fresh.

I think I have said enough about picnics, delectable as they always must be, unless sodden with rain and wind on a birdless grouse moor. The *change* is the magic. The hungry nomad surely gets no thrill – poor nomad!

Diana Cooper

A Birthday Picnic in the Piddle Valley

BEATRICE DEBENHAM

The end of the harvest and a birthday coincided rather happily, and we decided on a picnic amongst the straw bales in a field overlooking the water meadows. Since the picnic site was near to the house it was relatively painless to take the food straight from the kitchen table on large plates, the salmon trout in the fish kettle, covered with fennel, and to put them on the table made of four straw bales covered with a very big white tablecloth. Salmon trout should really be cooked as proper fishermen cook salmon, that is, wrapped up in greaseproof paper, covered with cold water in the fish kettle, brought very slowly to the boil, taken off at once and cooled in the water. This is foolproof unless the water is allowed to boil. We began our cooking too late for this method, so we covered the salmon trout with fennel, and put it on the tray of the fish kettle with a little water below, and steamed it for half an hour. The combination of smoked salmon followed by salmon trout was rather haphazard, but they both went very well with Mrs Tucker's gorse wine, which is a powerful brew.

The water meadows around Affpuddle in Dorset are some of the last in the Piddle Valley to be kept up in the old way with hatches, and flooded to keep the frost off the grass in order to give the cows an 'early bite'. They are also flooded when it gets dry in the summer, which infuriates neighbouring sportsmen, some of whom have busied themselves digging out trout pools, and hate the traditional floodings which upset their fish. Heated passions are aroused.

Our picnic was decorated halfway through by a frieze of cows ambling up to be milked. Cigarettes were scattered amongst the straw bales but nothing caught fire, and they kept the flies away. Finally the hazelnut chocolate birthday cake, as usual, left us all comatose.

Wholemeal Bread (Eliza's Loaf)

1 oz (25 g) sea salt (Maldon or Tidman's)
3½ lb (1 kg 575 g) stone-ground wholewheat flour
1 oz (25 g) yeast (or up to 4 oz [110 g] for extra value)
1 oz (25 g) Barbados brown sugar
2½ pints (1.5 litres) water at blood heat
Three medium bread tins

Mix the salt with the flour in a big bowl and warm it so that the yeast will work more quickly. Crumble the yeast in a pudding basin, add the sugar and ½ pint (275 ml) of the lukewarm water. Leave for 10 minutes or so to froth up, then stir to dissolve the sugar. Pour this yeasty liquid into the basin of flour together with the rest of the warm water. Stir it all with a wooden spoon until the flour is evenly wetted. Do not knead. Grease the tins, half fill with the dough and put in a warm place (i.e. a low oven or on top of an Aga) covered with a damp cloth.

Preheat the oven to gas mark 6 (400° F, 200° C). Leave the dough about 20 minutes to rise by one third. Bake for about 35 minutes or until the base of each loaf sounds hollow when removed from its tin and tapped. Cool on a wire tray.

Cecilia's Favourite Cake

12 oz (350 g) butter	
12 oz (350 g) sugar	
6 eggs	*To decorate*
6 oz (175 g) grated plain	1 lb (450 g) plain chocolate
chocolate or plain cocoa	Hazelnuts and marzipan
6 oz (175 g) self-raising flour	fruit, etc.

Preheat the oven to gas mark 6 (400° F, 200° C). Beat the butter to a cream, add the sugar, and beat well till creamy. Separate the eggs and add the yolks gradually to the mixture. Sift the flour and fold in gradually, together with the chocolate or cocoa. Whisk the egg whites to the soft peak stage, then fold into the mixture. Grease a 9-inch round cake tin, and bake the mixture for about 1½ hours. Stick a knife in near the end of the time – if it comes out clean the cake is cooked.

Turn out on a wire tray to cool, then carefully cut in two cross-ways. Grate the remaining chocolate, melt in a cup over a pan of hot (not boiling) water, and cover the top of the bottom half. Replace the top half and cover with chocolate in the same way. Decorate with marzipan fruit, mimosa balls, angelica leaves or halved hazelnuts.

Beatrice Debenham

Devonshire Picnic

JOSCELINE DIMBLEBY

Halfway up to Totnes on the River Dart there is a peninsula of majestic oak and beech trees; it has green sun-dappled banks and we know it as Picnic Point. Almost every day during the school holidays in Devon we picnic. We sail to coves along the coast, or we drive on to Dartmoor for long walks through forests, rewarded by a home-made pasty eaten on the mossy banks of a stream. On wild-weather days we row to the other side of the river by our house, to a disused quarry so sheltered from all winds by its cathedral-like walls that plants grow there of an exotic character quite unexpected in England. But Picnic Point is the most magical place of all. It has a natural fireplace on a promontory looking down into the deep green water, and although there are always signs of others having had a fire there shortly before, we have never, in all our years of Devon life, had to share Picnic Point with anyone.

The boat journey up the Dart is beautiful; most beautiful of all is the calm of early evening in the last yellow sunlight when we often sail up for a picnic supper. One evening we cooked a huge rib of beef – smoky, tender and rare – which we ate by the light of the fire while the children, inspired by the dark woods all round and the river noises, told ghost stories.

Our picnic cooking has been simplified by a large two-sided grill into which the food is clamped and turned over all at once – none of that endless forking of sausages while the smoke chokes and blinds you. We simply put stones on either side of the fire, balance the grill over it, and sit back sipping scrumpy and savouring the smell of the cooking. My children normally profess to dislike sausages, but good butchers' sausages cooked in the smoke of a driftwood fire and stuffed into a fresh bun roll with some mustard and crisp lettuce are always welcome. The other success on the grill is marinaded meat and chicken – the aroma of Indian spices wafting into the English country air has a nice incongruity, and a bold flavour is just what keen outdoor appetites need.

Sometimes when we have set out late we eat on the boat. Tastes are more exciting in the open air, so hot food seems extra special. I often stuff a mixture of grated cheese, onion and herbs, bound with whisked egg, into buttered baps; cook them, wrapped in foil, in a fairly high oven for 15–20 minutes before we leave the house; and wrap the foil up in layers of newspaper. They keep hot for hours, even in the chill of a sea breeze.

Our Devon picnics are an everyday affair. The food is appreciated as much as any I prepare, but the crowded summer days give one no time for elaborate preparation. The special-occasion picnic which I have time to think about, gives me the creative challenge I enjoy best. For Glyndebourne once I made a game pie decorated musically and inscribed with the words of the opera we were there for, *Così Fan Tutte*. When my children were small we used sometimes to take a large group of their friends for a birthday picnic tea and games in Richmond Park. It gave me great satisfaction to produce an array of brightly coloured cakes, jellies and biscuits set out on the grass on a large white sheet.

Then there are picnics abroad: often uncomfortable, hot, prickly, often not in the perfect spot, but more of a pleasure to shop for. In the East I have had wonderful picnics, prepared in grand, old-fashioned style. I remember one lunch sitting in basket chairs high up above the Ganges at Chunar in central India, eating delicate samosas, spicy meat balls and marinaded chicken out of a basket lined with starched white linen, as we watched and heard a panorama of life on the great river below us.

Having been brought up with all manner of picnics a major part of my life, our nautical Devon feasts have now become most familiar to me, and as a spot which has everything, even its own vegetable crop, the succulent samphire, growing on the mud at low tide, Picnic Point on the River Dart for us reigns supreme.

Grilled Spiced Chicken
(for 6–8)

I find this the most popular picnic food of all. All you have to do is remember to spare a few minutes the night before to prepare the delicious marinade, and in the morning the chicken pieces, tender and aromatic with Indian spices, will be ready to take on your picnic. They will cook well either over charcoal or on a simple grill over a wood fire. If you must, you can cook them in advance on your grill at home – in any case they are excellent cold. You can use any joints of chicken but I find inexpensive chicken wings very successful. Of course you can vary the spices according to what you have.

1½–2 lb (700–900 g) small chicken joints

For the Marinade
1 onion, sliced roughly
1-inch (2.5 cm) piece of fresh ginger,
    peeled and chopped roughly
6–8 cloves garlic, peeled
3 teaspoons ground coriander
2 teaspoons ground cinnamon
2 teaspoons ground cardamom
½ teaspoon chilli powder or cayenne
3 tablespoons red wine vinegar
3 tablespoons sunflower oil
1 tablespoon tomato purée
1 rounded teaspoon salt

Simply put all the marinade ingredients into a liquidizer or food processor and whizz to a smooth paste. Pour the marinade over the chicken joints, stir to coat thoroughly, and leave in a covered bowl in the refrigerator or a cool place overnight.

Grill over a high heat on both sides until almost blackened.

Beef and Onion Flatbreads
(for 5–6)

These are rather like a wholemeal pancake incorporating minced beef and onion. You can wrap them up in foil while they are hot and then in thick newspaper to keep them warm until you reach your picnic place. Alternatively you can eat them cold. Either way, take with you a box of cut lettuce, tomato and fresh mint leaves and wrap the flatbreads round a stuffing of this mixture. They are delicious and nutritious, and children love them too.

1 large onion
4 oz (110 g) minced beef
½–1 teaspoon chilli powder
12 oz (350 g) wholemeal or 85% wholewheat flour
Sunflower oil for frying
Salt

Peel the onion and chop very finely. Mix with the minced beef in a large bowl. Season with chilli powder and a generous sprinkling of salt. Add the flour and mix in with your hands. Gradually stir in up to ¼ pint (150 ml) water – enough to make the mixture stick together. Knead on a well-floured board for 3–4 minutes. Then take egg-sized handfuls of the dough and shape these into round balls. Sprinkle board and rolling pin with flour to prevent sticking, and roll out the dough as thinly as you can. Heat about ¼ inch (5 mm) oil in a large frying pan. Fry the breads one by one at a medium-to-high heat, turning once, until brown on each side. Drain on absorbent paper and pile on a serving dish in a very low oven to keep warm until you are ready to leave.

Pigeon Pie
(for 8–10)

This cold pie, rich with flavour, is perfect for a festive picnic. You can make it well in advance, but take it out of the refrigerator an hour or so before you eat it as the rich pastry tastes better when it is not too cold.

For the pastry	*For the filling*
12 oz (350 g) strong white flour	2 wood pigeons
1 teaspoon salt	12 oz (350 g) boned rabbit
8 oz (225 g) butter or margarine	8 oz (225 g) minced veal
2 tablespoons water	2 teaspoons fresh green peppercorns
1 egg	8–10 juniper berries, crushed (optional)
	1 bunch spring onions, cut into ½ inch (1 cm) lengths
	1 small carton soured cream
	Salt, black pepper

To make the pastry sift the flour and salt into a bowl. Gently melt the fat with the water in a saucepan. Then make a well in the flour and pour the melted fat and water in, stirring it into the flour with a spoon as you do so. Stir until it is evenly mixed, then beat the egg and add it. Mix vigorously to a smooth dough.

Cut all the flesh you can from the pigeons – I find I can get it off most easily by pulling it with my fingers – and cut it up roughly. Cut the boned rabbit up into small pieces, in a food processor if you have one. Put the pigeon, rabbit and veal in a bowl. Add the green peppercorns, the crushed juniper berries and the chopped spring onions. Stir in the soured cream and season with black pepper.

Butter well a 7½–8-inch cake tin with a push-up base. Take the pastry from the refrigerator and knead on a lightly floured board until pliable. Cut off a little under three-quarters of the pastry and roll out into a circle large enough to line the cake tin. (If the pastry breaks while you are lining the tin, don't worry, just press it together again.) Spoon the meat mixture into the pastry-lined tin and level the top. Turn back the overlapping edges of the pastry over the edge of the meat and moisten. Roll out the remaining pastry into a piece big enough to cover the top. Put the cake tin on top of the rolled out pastry and cut round the edge to make a perfect circle. Carefully place on top of the meat and press down the edges. Roll out the pastry trimmings to make decorations. Prick two or three holes in the pastry with a skewer, and if time put the pie in the fridge for 30 minutes or more before baking. Preheat the oven to gas mark 4 (350° F, 180° C).

Brush the top of the pie with milk, and cook in the centre of the oven for 1½–1¾ hours. Check the pie during cooking, and when the top looks brown enough lay a piece of foil on top. Leave the pie to become cold in the tin. Then carefully ease the edges off with a knife and push out. With a spatula, ease the pie off the base of the tin onto a bed of lettuce or other leaves on a serving plate.

Josephine Dunsleby

Missy Allen, 'An
American Indoor
Picnic': A Pic-nic in
the drawing room –
a capital thing for
a wet day
(Lent by Paul
Channon)
▽

◁ Harold Acton,
'Picnic at the Ming
Tombs'
(Anne Tennant)

Missy Allen: The Johnston family (Alexander Lindsay)

Carey Basset, 'Carey's Cold Collation' (Carey Basset) △
Jonathan Burnham, 'Gaveston Picnic, 1981' ▽

Nicholas Coleridge, 'Picnic
at the Grange'

Arabella Boxer, 'A Picnic for
the Air' (Violet Vyner)

Clementine Beit, 'Glory's Picnic'
(Felicity Todd)

Colette Clark, 'A Picnic in Portugal'. Left to right: Colette and Sam Clark with Irene Worth (Julian Sainsbury)

Valeria Coke, 'A Picnic by the Fountain of Perseus and Andromeda, Holkham, Norfolk' The Coke family (Anne Tennant)

George Christie, 'Glyndebourne: A Critical View of the Picnic' (Anne Tennant)

Silvia Combe, 'Holkham Beach Picnic'. Left to right: Lady Coke,
Silvia Coke (the author), David Coke and Miss Langran

Silvia Combe, 'Picnic with the Poles, 1941'. Left: Miss Kitty Combe,
right: Lady Silvia Combe

Beatrice Debenham, 'A Birthday Picnic in the Piddle Valley'
(Beatrice Debenham)

Diana Gage, 'The English Picnic.' Left to right: David Herbert, Bridet Parsons, Diana Gage, Caroline and Teresa Jungman, Tilly Losch, Tony Herbert, Cecil Beaton and Betty Smith
(Cecil Beaton)

Desmond Doig, 'When Abominable Snowmen went Picnicking' (Desmond Doig)

Jasper Guinness, 'Whoopee Picnic' (Anne Tennant)

Ian Graham, 'Picnic in Guatemala' (Ian Graham)

◁ Josceline Dimbleby,
'Devonshire Picnic'

Milton Gendel, 'Picnic in
Rome'. Left to right:
Evelyn Waugh, Diana
Cooper and Georgina
Masson (Milton
Gendel)
▽

Min Hogg, 'Autumn Mushroom Picnic'. Left to right: Lady Diana Cooper, Nicky Haslam and Min Hogg (Min Hogg)

Dme Heinz, 'A New England Clambake' (Charles Adams) ▽

Derek Hill; 'A Painter's Picnic' (Derek Hill)

When Abominable Snowmen Went Picnicking

DESMOND DOIG

My favourite picnic story comes from Sherpa country below Mount Everest and is about 250 years old. That was the time when the area fairly crawled with yetis or abominable snowmen. They became a nuisance, particularly as one of their pastimes was carrying off beautiful young women. In a village called Khumjung, from which some of the most famous Sherpas come, yetis became so thick on the ground that they got in the way. They preyed on precious yaks, dug up valuable potato fields and made the nights alarming with their high-pitched screaming and whistling. Besides, they smelled and were bad-tempered.

The most wise and wily Sherpa elders got together in a series of drunken conferences. How could they rid themselves of the yetis, remembering that they themselves were good Buddhists and couldn't slay the beasts, and that there were some, particularly the lamas, who considered the abominable creatures to be more holy than undesirable.

Unfortunately the person who thought up the prizewinning idea has long since been forgotten. It was, remember, a boozy gathering. The Sherpas of Khumjung, it was decided, would go on one of their popular picnics. Great bowls of potato beer were made by the village ladies, and even more potent bowls of doped *rakshi*, or potato spirit. There were also enough meat dumplings, called *momos*, to build a large house. The curious yetis watched as the villagers, dressed in their brocaded and woolly best, took off to a clearing on a hill nearby and there set to feasting and drinking. Obviously they thought nothing about the fact that every man carried two swords, one made of wood, the other the real thing.

When the Sherpas had had their fill of food and drink, they began to gamble, and then fell to fighting. Wooden swords were drawn and almost every man was 'killed'. Death had never been so noisy and dramatic. Some victims threshed about so much that they almost landed in the river thousands of feet below. Women joined in, torn between lamentation and chopping each other up. The yetis looked on in amazement until it was almost dark. By then the few Sherpas left 'alive' had been dragged by the 'survivors' to their huts. The great pots of doped spirits and hundreds of genuine sharpened swords were left behind. Now it was time for the yetis to have their picnic and, being powerful mimics, it was not long before they feasted and drank, then made a pretence at playing and finally fell upon each other with the swords abandoned by the 'dead' Sherpas.

Great was the slaughter as each side whistled up reinforcements from the dark surrounding mountains, and yetis of all sizes and sexes hurled themselves into the fray. Just a few remained to clear up the battlefield as the Sherpas had done. But when morning came three yeti corpses still remained to be cleared away, and it was on these that the Sherpas descended and removed their scalps as relics to be kept in the village monasteries.

The scalps are still there, in the Sherpa monasteries of Khumjung, Pangboche and Namc Bazar, where they are looked upon with a certain awe and reverence. For years they baffled mountaineers and scientists to whom a few hairs filched from the scalps were sent. The Khumjung scalp became one of the most important clues in the hunt for the elusive snowmen.

In 1960 the mountaineer Sir Edmund Hillary, an eminent American zoologist named Marlin Perkins, and I borrowed the scalp on pain of several very horrid deaths and took it to Chicago, New York, London and Paris. Quite a picnic! It was declared a fake, made from the hide of a wild goat.

Does this mean the epic Sherpa and yeti picnic didn't really happen? It's almost like declaring the Tower of London nonexistent if the Crown Jewels turn out to be fakes.

Momos
(Tibetan Meat Dumplings)

1 oz (25 g) yeast	1 onion, chopped
1 teaspoon sugar	Salt
1½ lb (700 g) plain flour	Pepper
8 oz (225 g) minced beef	1 tablespoon olive oil

Dissolve the yeast in a cup of warm water with the sugar. Mix with the flour and knead into a dough. Put in a warm place until the dough rises (about 3–4 hours.)

Divide the dough into a dozen portions and, using flour to prevent it sticking, roll each portion into a flat round shape about 3 inches (7.5 cm) in diameter.

Meanwhile mix the minced beef with the chopped onion and seasoning and oil and work it into a stuffing. Take a piece of dough and place a piece of this stuffing in the centre. Turn up the sides of the dough to wrap around the stuffing until only a small opening is left at the top; pinch this opening together. Place all the uncooked dumplings in a hot steamer and steam for about 20 minutes.

Desmond Doig

A Scottish Family Picnic

JENNY FRASER

'Picnic!' The word explodes through the house followed by a scramble for the telephone to summon as many friends and relations as can be lured into the trap. Usually about thirty. In the Highlands, always warmer out than in, nothing short of a deluge will cancel a picnic once the idea is mooted. The children look forward to an opportunity for an uproarious party and the exhausted hostess to a remission from the tyranny of the Aga cooker.

Vital to the success of the expedition are a couple of gargantuan frying pans. Next on the list are two spatulas, breadboard, knife for spreading and fork for prodding. An old cardboard box is rapidly filled with the familiar ingredients: eggs, Ayrshire bacon, sausages and beefburgers, of which we usually have ample supplies made up in advance. A mixture of well-seasoned mince with finely sliced onions, garlic, fresh parsley, thyme and a pinch of nutmeg is the most popular recipe. Tomato ketchup, beloved of the under-tens, and a jar of Branston pickle for the teenagers must be included. Large quantities of fresh baps, Islay cheese, fruit and a bag of small, hard tomatoes complete the picnic fare. Drinks normally consist of orange squash, cider and a generous supply of supermarket wine.

All this is hastily thrust into the boot of the car, together with coats and fishing macs. The Spartans among us grab bathing suits and towels. Three hoots on the car horn and everyone hurtles out of the house to be counted and squeezed into half a dozen cars. We're off!

It goes without question that we are on our way to a scene of great beauty which will include waterfall, loch and old Caledonian forest.

Once there, after a drive of up to an hour, everyone down to the four-year-old must carry something through the knee-high heather and ubiquitous bracken. At the chosen spot all gather wood, and the genius who has remembered the matches takes charge. Two chief cooks and a chief spreader are appointed. Volunteers for the former are not lacking but half an hour over a blazing fire, eyes streaming from the wayward smoke, while taking orders for underdone hamburgers, bacon burnt to a frazzle and eggs in every conceivable state of liquidity soon palls. Output from the frying pan speeds up and assistant butter spreaders are dragooned into service. When every mouth is finally filled we relax, open the wine and, drowning as best we can the taste of smoke and cinders, lie back midge-bitten in the heather. It is probably beginning to rain but it is more than your life is worth to mention it. The supermarket wine, by now superb vintage claret, has done its work, and we don't care.

The culmination of the day is the plunge, or push, into the loch. Wild bets are thrown out on who will be the first to cross. Honour satisfied, we gather our belongings and head home.

If we anticipate staying out all day, someone throws together this last-minute recipe for scones for about twenty.

Scones

1 lb (450 g) self-raising flour
1 teaspoon bicarbonate of
  soda
2 teaspoons cream of tartar
1 pinch of salt
1 tablespoon golden syrup
2 eggs
Milk and water

Preheat the oven to gas mark 8 (450° F, 230° C). Sieve together the dry ingredients into a bowl, then beat the eggs and add along with the golden syrup and enough milk and water to make a dough. Roll out on a floured surface to about 1 inch (2.5 cm) thick, cut into rounds and bake for 5 minutes. Wrap in cooking foil when cooked, to keep warm.

Jenny Fraser

The English Picnic

DIANA GAGE

It was in the springtime long ago, over the bare downs, along the ridge, then a sudden descent by a rough track – hawthorns in flower, a burbling stream, singing birds, murmuring insects and an exquisite, fantastical house sited at the end of a remote valley.

Not an inconoclast's idea of an English picnic – sand in the tea, stones in the sea, freezing fog, crying children, tired legs, aching arms, ants, mosquitoes, wasps, swooping gulls, rapacious goats, inquisitive cows, incipient bulls. Recently a visiting professor confessed in an unwary moment that he wished to observe English life, and was subjected to most of these hazards. He was kind enough to say he appreciated the experience, but added that he did not wish to repeat it.

The particular picnic that I recall from so long ago was not typically English at all – a mixture of nationalities, sitting in perfect comfort a few yards from the house. The feast spread on a snowy tablecloth; a charming uniformed parlourmaid pouring out from a silver teapot. Our host set the camera and joined the group; a moment in time had been preserved.

Memory has retained even the details of the food: the thinnest of brown bread, cucumber sandwiches, brandy snaps, éclairs, chocolate cake, elderflower fritters, candied lemon and orange peel – even a sorbet. There was no significance, nothing much happened. We were young, we were friends, we enjoyed each other's company. It is nearly half a century ago – but it is engraved in the archives of memory in letters of pure gold.

Gooseberry and Elderflower Sorbet

1 pint (570 ml) water   A handful of elderflowers
8 oz (225 g) white sugar   Juice of 4 lemons
1 lb (450 g) gooseberries   Whipped cream

Put the water and sugar in a pan and boil, stirring to make a syrup. Add the gooseberries and elderflowers. Remove from heat. Cover the pan and let it stand for a couple of hours. Strain. Add the lemon juice and whipped cream. Freeze.

Brandy Snaps

4 oz (110 g) butter
8 oz (225 g) golden syrup
6 oz (175 g) sugar
5 oz (150 g) self-raising flour
1–2 teaspoons ground ginger

Preheat the oven to gas mark 4 (350° F, 180° C). Put the butter, treacle and sugar into a pan, melt, then stir in gradually the flour and ginger. Mix well. Roll into small balls when cold, put on a warm, buttered baking sheet and bake for 20 minutes. When nearly cold, roll round the handle of a wooden spoon and twist into hollow cylinders. Fill with whipped cream.

Candied Lemon or Orange Peel

Orange or lemon peel, pith removed
2 lb (900 g) white sugar
2 pints (1 litre 150 ml) water

To make the syrup, bring the sugar and water to boiling point in a pan. Blanch the peel in another pan of boiling water. Add the peel to the syrup and leave overnight. Remove the peel and boil the syrup until it drops off a spoon in a short thread. Put back the peel, and repeat the whole process two or three times. The syrup should eventually crystallize.

Diana Sage

Picnic in Rome

MILTON GENDEL

For generations the English have been domesticating the Sublime by choosing its precincts for their picnics. There is no beauty spot in creation, on Alp, lakeside or riverbank, in jungle or desert, that has not served as a setting for a group of English people with picnic baskets, spirit lamps and teapots in cosies. At least this was so before the highway picnic became current, with picnickers on folding chairs and the open boot of the car serving as buffet.

Once, in the spring, a few decades ago, Rome offered a happy conjunction of scenic sublimity and picnicking English to provide appropriate foreground figures. Evelyn Waugh, in the Holy City for his annual Easter devotions, was the star of the occasion. Jenny Crosse, daughter of Robert Graves and correspondent of *Picture Post*, was always the moving spirit on such occasions. She rang up Babs Johnson, the writer known as Georgina Masson.

'Evelyn Waugh is here with Diana Cooper – you know – she's Mrs Stitch in his novels. I thought we might have it at your place.'

The self-educated daughter of an Indian Army officer, Babs brought the competence, pertinacity and inspiration of a Mrs Beeton to her various interests. The two ladies devised the guest list, which contained enough flannel-coated men and hatted or bandanna-ed women to provide the cast for a proper English picnic.

Then Evelyn Waugh announced that he would come to the picnic only if he did not have to sit on the ground. With some regret Babs Johnson gave up the thought of the remoter romantic glades of the villa, where daffodils were springing and cherry trees blossoming, and moved her tables and chairs out in front of the vaulted stable that old Prince Filippo Doria let her have as a grace-and-favour home in his park.

A lovely limpid blue and gold April day framed Babs's stable-yard rock garden. Jenny bustled about serving Frascati, mascarpone and ricotta seasoned with salt and pepper and garnished with a sprinkling of paprika. Next came tufted raw fennel, to be pulled apart and dipped in olive oil with mustard, and eggs stuffed with anchovies. Round loaves of crusty bread, the descendants of those found – baked hard – in the ashes of Pompeii were set out together with plates of prosciutto, minuscule slices of spicy salami, rounds of lonza and mortadella.

When Evelyn Waugh arrived he was allotted a little table to himself where he sat plump with a commanding air, more lordly than any rank-proud gentleman on the Grand Tour.

The talk turned on the personality and history of Pius XII, the reigning pontiff. Jenny and Babs were censorious. The Pope was austere, autocratic. Sympathetic to German *Kultur*, he had not been outspoken enough against the Nazis. True, the Vatican had contributed to the gold ransom extorted from the Roman Jews during the German occupation, but it hadn't prevented their deportation or the massacre of the hostages at the Fosse Ardeatine. A devout Catholic guest blushed with discomfiture at the protracted and irreverent discussion. Evelyn Waugh, now impatient, banged his fork on the table.

Jenny placatingly held out a bottle of Frascati.

'Some wine, Evelyn?' He fixed her with a cold blue eye. 'Mrs Crosse,' he said, with compelling emphasis, 'has anyone ever remarked on the uncanny resemblance between you and the late unlamented Mrs Roosevelt? Undoubtedly she was one of the most ill-favoured women the world has ever seen.'

A stunned silence followed this pronouncement, as its author returned to spearing rounds of salami. It was broken by Diana Cooper, out of the depths of her bonnet: 'He's just *too* awful.'

Jenny retreated to the stable converted into a sitting-room where Babs was uncorking some wine. 'Are you crying?' Babs asked. Jenny repeated what had just been said to her. Babs, a sturdy woman with iron-grey hair, a determined look and a kind eye, listened with growing indignation. She had been brought up near the Khyber Pass, where respect was paid to the New Testament on Sundays and holidays, but where daily life was ruled more by the Old Testament. She was also uncompromising in her view of women's rights.

'Jenny,' she said, 'you go right out there now and hit him as hard as you can. You're a woman and he won't dare hit you back.' Jenny looked shocked, but obediently turned and went back to the rock garden.

Evelyn Waugh peered up at her with a bland expression as she addressed him: 'Evelyn, I have always admired you as a writer. After your behaviour today I want you to know that I no longer admire you as a man. But, as Christians, perhaps we meet on common ground. So I *forgive* you.'

As a master of dry comedy he must have relished the turning of his elective worm into a monument of moral dignity. The company certainly did: there were shouts of laughter, followed by praise for Jenny and belated reproval for Evelyn Waugh.

'I don't care much for picnics,' said Waugh when it was time to go. 'But I enjoyed this one immensely. And I shall never forget it.'

Anchovy Eggs

Eggs	
Mayonnaise	Lemon juice
Anchovy fillets	Mustard
Salt	Cayenne
Pepper	Basil

Hard-boil the eggs. Crack the shells and drop immediately into cold water to minimize the darkening of the yolks. Shell and cut in halves lengthwise. Mash the yolks and moisten with mayonnaise and well-pounded anchovy fillets. Season to taste with salt, pepper, lemon juice, mustard and cayenne. Refill the whites with this mixture and sprinkle with chopped basil.

Milton Gendel

Picnic in Guatemala

IAN GRAHAM

On hearing that I take all my meals out of doors during several months of the year, and that I generally eat them sitting on the ground in a forest, you might suppose me to be either mad, or a keen and expert picnicker. Alas, as a picnicker I am neither keen nor expert. My apparent mania for al fresco dining is no more than a consequence of the kind of archaeological work I undertake in Guatemala, and the meals that I provide are decidedly not good picnic fare. Far from being fresh and appetizing in appearance, or made up with a due proportion of vegetables and fruit into unusual, perhaps even surprising, dishes, mine are nearly always stodgy affairs in which rice, black beans and tortillas routinely play the leading roles, and they are mostly devoured in a perfunctory way during respites from work. Unfortunately, fruit and vegetables soon rot in the tropical heat, and before an expedition is two weeks old they have disappeared from the menu.

Even a French explorer seems to have despaired of the available materials. In describing a journey through these same regions a century ago, Désiré Charnay gives a menu: it starts with *soupe d'haricots noirs* and goes on predictably to *haricots noirs rissolés*, but his *vin de Bordeaux* must have made the meal more bearable. Evidently his mule train clanked along to the music of wine bottles, one of which I even found, still unbroken, near a waterhole by which he must have camped. I imagine that in spite of the poor provender, strict etiquette was observed, even in that sweltering jungle; a photograph shows his secretary properly dressed in a frock-coat.

Still, I *have* sometimes tried to provide a picnic worthy of the name for a visitor, particularly one who has brought in fresh supplies. And in the absence of such supplies there is always a chance of finding something growing in the forest that will contribute freshness and crunch, one of the most delicious being heart of palm. But to obtain this one has to find a tree at just the right stage of growth, and fell it with an axe.

Of these more ambitious picnics, some may be counted successful. At least none has been more unsuccessful as the one mentioned so laconically in *Lolita*. Humbert Humbert, you may remember, tells us that his 'very photogenic mother died in a freak accident (picnic, lightning)'. Nor have any of us yet been struck down by ptomaine poisoning. In this connection, though, I do offer a word of caution that is as relevant to picnics on hot days in temperate climates as it is to the tropics: avoid making up sandwiches or other food with mayonnaise or soft cheese, both of which suit the taste of bacteria all too well. On the other hand, dressings made acid with vinegar or lemon juice put them off.

The photograph records a picnic that might have been successful but for one small mishap. It was held in a ruined city of the ancient Maya called La Pasadita, a very small one consisting of only a few public buildings perched on a steep hill with vertical rock faces on two sides. Only one building remains standing, and even this seems doomed to collapse at any moment. Until some fifteen years ago the doorways were spanned by beautifully carved stone lintels, then these were wrenched out by looters. Inside, the walls show the remains of fresco painting, with portraits of rulers and scenes of ceremony. The main elements of our not very sumptuous picnic were: black bean and chorizo salad, empanadas, flour tortillas, mangoes and lemonade.

Black Beans and Chorizo Salad

8 oz (225 g) black beans or (much better) lentils	Black olives
1¾ pints (1 litre) water	1 teaspoon salt
Chorizo or other spicy sausage	Olive oil
1 large onion	Wine vinegar
	French mustard

Wash the beans or lentils, bring to the boil and cook, but do not allow them to become mushy. Drain. Cut the sausage into cubes, add chopped onion, chopped black olives and salt and blend with the lentils. Before serving, pour over a dressing of olive oil, vinegar and French mustard.

Empanadas
(makes about 15)

Pastry
12 oz (350 g) self-raising flour
½ teaspoon salt
4 oz (110 g) butter
1 egg yolk
2 tablespoons milk for glaze

Filling
1 lb (450 g) minced beef, or
  pork and beef (wild boar
  when I made them at La
  Pasadita)

1 tablespoon olive oil
1 small onion, chopped
1 clove garlic, crushed
1 tomato, peeled and chopped
2 tablespoons chopped
  blanched almonds
½ teaspoon chilli powder
6 dessertspoons raisins
6 green olives, pitted and
  sliced
2 teaspoons capers

Put the flour and salt in a bowl. Cut in the butter until thoroughly mixed. Gradually add enough iced water to form a dough. Wrap the dough in plastic film and keep in the refrigerator while you make the filling.

Heat the oil in frying pan and cook the meat until no longer pink, stirring the while. Add onion, garlic, tomato, almonds, chilli powder, raisins (previously soaked in hot water if hard), olives and capers. Cook over reduced heat for 6–8 minutes, stirring frequently. Add salt to taste. If the mixture is still wet, cook longer. Cool.

Preheat the oven to gas mark 5 (375° F, 190° C). Roll out the dough on a floured surface to rather less than ⅛ inch (3 mm) thick. Cut in squares of about 4 inches (10 cm). Place a tablespoon of the filling in each square, then fold over on the diagonal, and crimp the edges together with your fingertips. Place the empanadas on greased baking tins and brush with a glaze prepared by beating the egg yolk with the milk. Bake for 15–20 minutes until golden. Place on a rack to cool.

Lemonade

A subtly different flavour can be imparted to lemonade by boiling up the lemon peel in it.

Postscript

As it turned out we were not to enjoy the empanadas, so laboriously baked in an improvised oven in our camp near La Pasadita. I left them during the morning hung in a plastic bag on a tree, out of reach of ants; but some animal, probably a large member of the stoat family, enjoyed them instead. So we had to make do with sardines. The table that can be seen in the photograph deserves a comment: it is all that is left of the lintel from the doorway in the background, its surface left smooth by the saw used to cut off the original carved surface.

Ian Graham

The Picnics of the Ancient Romans

MICHAEL GRANT

Julius Caesar followed up the celebration of his Triumphs over his enemies by presiding – sweating profusely, we are told – over an open-air dinner in the public squares of Rome, attended by many tens if not hundreds of thousands of Romans who drank a good Italian wine (Falernian) and ate, among other things, six thousand eels 'lent' to Caesar by a former political opponent. The dictator liked doing things on a large scale, and this may have been the biggest picnic of all time (picnic? Yes, according to the *Concise Oxford Dictionary*, 'pleasure party including meal out of doors').

Queen Cleopatra did not attend Caesar's party because she was not in Rome, although she arrived shortly afterwards. But if she had been at the dinner she would surely have felt like one of her royal Greek forbears, Queen Arsinoe III of Egypt, who described the picnickers at Alexandria's Feast of Flagons as 'a squalid kind of party – a mixed crowd gorging up stale food'. Arsinoe would scarcely have been better pleased if she had attended some of the numerous similar festivals in Italy, which gave the opportunity for a good deal of fairly unrestrained eating and drinking. For example at the annual Festival of Anna Perenna, on 15 March, people camped out with their girlfriends in tents or huts of leafy boughs or reeds, and everyone drank themselves silly. At the Hilaria, the spring festival of the Great Mother, it was the custom to offer the goddess an extraordinarily pungent, garlicky salad ('its powerful whiff smites the nostrils', remarked a poet), and no doubt the revellers ate the leftovers. But it was at the various Italian harvest and grape harvest celebrations that the most extensive open-air eating and drinking took place. The emperor Elagabalus once took his court to one of these wine festivals. An outdoor occasion of such a kind did not, perhaps, give him an opportunity for some of his most exquisite alleged touches of banqueting humour, such as letting down a mass of violets and other flowers from the ceiling in such quantities that the guests were smothered to death, but nevertheless we are given a lively account of the coarse talk with which he saw fit to enliven the occasion.

The shepherds in Virgil's *Eclogues* invest the idea of *déjeuner sur l'herbe* with a far more idyllic, romantic glow. However, the *Eclogues* were written not for shepherds but for highly sophisticated Romans: and such Romans, although they were prepared to read about such matters – and had (indoors) adopted the uncomfortable eastern and Greek practice of eating lying down – would mostly have endured almost any torture rather than share the discomforts of what we understand by a picnic. After all, one did not *have* to eat completely out of doors. True, as recent discoveries have shown, it was possible to eat at pleasant little dining-places in a Pompeii vineyard, under a pergola. But the architects of the grand houses and villas in the area were adept at distributing a number of indoor dining-rooms, suited to the various seasons, at various strategic points of the building, including summer rooms that were *very nearly* out of doors, opening alluringly upon elegant gardens (not upon untutored nature, except for the occasional seascape). A rich, fastidious late Roman, Sidonius Apollinaris, describes such a room, though while gushing about the view he also does not fail to mention a 'glittering sideboard' – and a staircase especially designed to avoid the slightest physical exertion.

However an earlier Roman, Pliny the Younger, at his country house on the borders of Tuscany and Umbria, actually entertained in his garden, completely al fresco, beside a marble basin filled with water: 'The preliminaries and main dishes for dinner are placed on the edge of the basin, while the lighter ones float about in vessels shaped like birds or little boats.' (Presumably slaves stood around with rakes to pull them in.) For whenever Romans could be lured outside to eat in the open air, they rather liked to have a watery setting. In the reign of Claudius, for example, a lot of people dined out to help the emperor celebrate the opening of a channel between a lake and a river. But the water overflowed, the picnickers got the shock of their lives, and the sponsor of the project ran into trouble.

More successful, in its way, was a rather unusual outdoor party given by Nero's appalling adviser Tigellinus on an artificial lake (or, according to another account, in a theatre specially flooded for the purpose). Tacitus reported it thus:

The entertainment took place on a raft, towed about by other vessels, with gold and ivory fittings. Their gay oarsmen were assorted according to age and speciality. Tigellinus had also collected birds and animals from remote countries, and even the creatures of the ocean. On the quays were brothels stocked with high-ranking ladies. Opposite them could be seen naked prostitutes, indecently posturing and gesturing. At nightfall, the woods and houses nearby echoed with singing and blazed with lights. . . .

The Romans, if they had to picnic, also liked to use grottoes or caves for the purpose. Some garden dining-rooms at Pompeii are artfully designed to look as if that was what they were. But you could also eat in real caves. The Emperor Tiberius did this on one occasion, with results even more disastrous than those which usually attend picnics: a fall of rock occurred that would have killed him, if his friend Sejanus had not interposed his body as a shield – an action that proved beneficial to his future career.

The wine drunk at these out-of-door meals, or indeed at any Roman party, was quite likely to include a tincture not only of resin (as in Greece today) or lime or even ashes (to counteract acidity) but also salt, almonds or goats' milk (to add maturity and flavour); and it was always possible that a red-hot iron had been dipped in it as well, for the same purpose. One also wonders, scanning the pages of Petronius' *Dinner of Trimalchio* and the scarcely less startling *Cookery Book of Apicius*, whether any of the more peculiar dishes described in these works made their appearance at a Roman picnic. Certainly, whatever meat or fish was provided, it would not have been served in any simple form (this elaborateness was no trouble to a Roman cook, who habitually produced his results, however complicated, on mobile, portable, sometimes unroofed charcoal stoves and tripods and gridirons).

Before sewing up your roast dormouse, for example, you ought to stuff it with minced pork and pound it with pepper, pine kernels, asafoetida or 'stinking mastic' (resinous gum smelling of garlic) and *liquamen. Liquamen* was the basis of *garum*, one of the very sharp sauces with which the Romans liked to drench every dish, partly because things went bad so quickly. According to one of its recipes, *garum* consisted basically of the chopped, pounded and crushed entrails of sprats and sardines, beaten into a fermented pulp (this is *liquamen*), which was left to evaporate for six weeks and then filtered through a perforated basket into a receptacle. The poet Martial, casting around for words to describe a friend's bad breath, can only remark that it would make even the strongest scent stink like *garum*; here, at least, is one argument in favour of outdoor picnics.

Martial speaks of fans of peacock feathers to keep flies away. But to the Emperor Domitian the flies that are always such a bore at picnics might actually have been an incentive to join in, because he liked having them around, amusing himself by catching them and cutting them to pieces with a specially sharpened metal pen. However, a picnic would not have been a possible milieu for his well-known party joke – serving the petrified senators who were his guests with black dishes and miniature gravestones inscribed with their names – because this inimitably humorous prank required indoor accommodation, with ceiling, walls and floor painted an equally funereal black. However, the insertion of Domitian into a discussion of picnics is probably irrelevant, since that emperor is even less likely than most other prominent Romans ever to have gone on one – and certainly not on a water picnic, since we are told that although he enjoyed solitary walks there were certain outdoor noises, notably the splash of oars, that he found intolerably irritating.

Michael Grant

Whoopee Picnic

JASPER GUINNESS

Nothing I like more than a picnic. Easily planned, but when the day dawns, I find, one does not always feel exactly one's best. But it's 'yoydleoy' and down to the market we go. First stop: the butcher. I've always been fond of spare ribs, unlike the Italians. They don't set much store by them and, as a result, they damn near give them away. The key word is *'rosticciana'*. Then off to the greengrocer for potatoes, lettuce, tomatoes, lemons and, most important, a huge water melon (*cocomero*).

Now, as Sherlock's friend asked him, 'Where do we buy the ingredients for the sauce?' *'Alimentari*, my dear Watson.' Sherlock's shop has the advantage of selling not only honey, oil, bread, tomato ketchup, butter and cheese, all of which are to be snapped up on the spot, but also rum, vodka and Cointreau, which are vital for the good of the water melon.

Home immediately. Time to get someone else to make the salad, the dressing, to wrap the potatoes in foil, and to make the sweet and sour sauce. Time for me to make the Bomba and collect some wood. Time for everyone to have a Camp. Sod. Good Lord. Here they come. Where's the wheelbarrow? Pile it all in, escort them to wherever we're going, light the fire, settle them down, give them a drink and have a lovely time.

Spare ribs: on the grill.

Sweet and sour sauce: take tomato ketchup (Heinz is best), squeezed lemons, honey, rosemary, and anything else in the cupboard.

Potatoes: wrap in silver foil and bung on the fire.
Salad and dressing: search me.

Bomba

Slice the very top off a big water melon. Take out the inside with a spoon and your hands. Squidge the insides through a colander into a pot. For a big melon put one bottle of rum, one of vodka and a little Cointreau into the empty shell of the fruit. Add as much of the juice as will fit in, leaving room for ice. Vary strength as seen fit.

Russian Picnic

LARISSA HASKELL

Russian literature is full of poetical descriptions of food. The jolly noise of pots and pans from the kitchen follows like a musical accompaniment to the idyllic childhood of Llijusha Oblomov in Goncharov's famous novel. Succulent meals of the rich Volga merchants make a reading of Melinikov-Pechersky's novel unbearable on an empty stomach. The joys of good food are celebrated on many pages of Anton Chekhov's stories, but nowhere as vividly as in 'Siren', where a clerk's lusty dream of a festive dinner drives everyone in the office crazy.

What about picnics? A reader who is looking for a menu is likely to be disappointed here – a furtive kiss in the woods would be easier to find. But the essence of a picnic – the special pleasure of eating on grass among the trees – is nowhere expressed better than in Tolstoy's *Childhood, Boyhood, Youth*.

When we reached Kalinovoe woods, we found the carriage already there, and, beyond all our expectations, a cart, in the midst of which sat the butler. In the shade we beheld a samovar, a cask with a form of ice-cream, and some other attractive parcels and baskets. It was impossible to make any mistake: there was to be tea, ice-cream and fruits in the open air. At the sight of the cart we manifested an uproarious joy; for it was considered a great treat to drink tea in the woods on the grass, and especially in a place where nobody had ever drunk tea before.

Chapter VII, translated by Isabel F. Hapgood

But if a picnic, seen through the eyes of a child, did not leave other memories than ice cream and fruit, the meal eaten by Natasha Rostov after the hunt in *War and Peace* is surprising both in its length and in its colourful description.

Liquors made from herbs, pickles, mushrooms, hot rye cakes, honey in the comb, foaming honey mead, apples, nuts both fresh and roasted and nuts in honey. . . . Preserves made with honey and others made with sugar, ham and freshly roasted chicken. . . .

Translated by Constance Garnett

A meal which would give many an idea to lovers of health food.

Picnics of course become especially popular with the growth of urban life, which adds a value to nature unpolluted by the presence of human beings, and so picnics have become a necessary part of recreation in present-day Russia both for the family and the courting couple seeking privacy. The favourite food is a shish kebab (called *shashlik*), cooked on charcoal in a hole dug into the earth, washed down by great quantities of vodka. I give here a few recipes which, while they are still popular today, could easily have been found in the picnic baskets of Tolstoy or Chekhov.

Pirojki with Spring Onions and Egg

Dough	*Filling*
¼ oz (7 g) fresh yeast	1 lb (450 g) spring onions
1 glass warm milk	Butter
1 lb (450 g) plain flour	2 hard-boiled eggs,
1 tablespoon melted butter	chopped

To make the dough, dissolve the yeast in the milk. Mix this liquid with the flour and melted butter and leave in a warm place to double in size (no kneading is required). Preheat the oven to gas mark 6 (400° F, 200° C). When ready, cut the dough into eight portions. Mix all the filling ingredients together. Fill each portion of dough with the mixture, seal and bake for one hour. Pirojki should serve as an accompaniment to the main course, for which I propose the following.

Kurinie Kotleti
Chicken Cutlets (serves four)

2 boned chicken breasts
1 slice white bread
Milk
1 egg
Oil for frying

Mince the chicken breasts. Soak the bread in milk and beaten egg and then mix with the chicken. Roll into little balls and fry in a frying pan in hot oil for 20 minutes. The essential thing is not to let the liquid escape.

Larissa Haswell

Picnic in China

MARY HAYLEY BELL

The earliest picnics I remember were in China before the Second World War. To us children they were something very special. My grandmother used to tell of picnics in Shanghai, with as many as twelve coolie helpers, and guests riding on ponies to the beautiful canal by their house, Unkaza, where a vast curry was served with chutneys, popadoms, shrimps and coconuts, not to mention sweets and coffee.

We had wonderful picnics during our childhood in Macao, where my father was Commissioner of Chinese Customs. He had two small armed launches in order to combat smuggling and gun-running. We used to go aboard preceded by the dining-room and kitchen staff who carried the food in large canisters, and crates of beer and wine. There would probably be about twenty guests. The anchor would be hauled up, and we would set out for Bias Bay, near Hong Kong. The lunch would probably consist of Chinese food: egg flower soup, deep-fried walnut chicken, paper-wrapped beef with shredded cabbage, fresh shrimp and lobster sauce, fried and boiled rice, crab-meat, glazed apples and pancakes. Everyone ate with chopsticks – in fact, my earliest memories of food are of eating with chopsticks.

Before 'Tiffin' as it was called in the East, we would have a swim from the *Pak Tow* or *Lung Tsing* – whichever launch we were in – while the Chinese crew stood by the machine-guns watching for pirates – for pirates there were. After half an hour's siesta we would be rowed ashore to the white gleaming beach of Leper Island, with the mountains behind and a distant view of Hong Kong.

Egg Flower Soup

2 pints (1 litre 150 ml) bone stock	1 teaspoon salt
	2 tablespoons soya sauce
2 eggs	½ teaspoon Ve-tsin
Vegetable oil	1 teaspoon vinegar
2 spring onions, chopped	Pepper

Bring the stock to the boil and remove from the heat. Beat the eggs, mix with a little oil, and pour slowly into the stock. Add the chopped onions and salt and bring to the boil again. Add soya sauce (or Ve-sop), Ve-tsin, vinegar and pepper. Stir with a ladle and it is ready to serve. The beaten eggs separate into hundreds of little threads on contact with the hot stock, which gives the soup its name.

Crabmeat in Steamed Eggs

1 large crab	
2 eggs	2 spring onions, chopped
1 teaspoon salt	2 tablespoons sherry
1 tablespoon soya sauce	1 tablespoon lard

Wash the crab and steam for 15 minutes. Remove the meat from the shell. Beat the eggs and mix them with the salt, soya sauce and chopped spring onions. Add the crabmeat, sherry and half a cup of water. Mix thoroughly and add lard. Steam for 20 minutes. It should be the consistency of thick cream. Put in a large thermos and serve with plain rice.

Mary Harbottle Bell

A New England Clambake

DRUE HEINZ

By far the messiest of all picnics is the famous American institution called the clambake or, before the price of lobster flew too high out of the water, the lobsterbake. In the twenties and thirties it was entirely different, and even grand. The famous Marshall Field, for instance, would anchor his great yacht off a beautiful stretch of beach in Maine and instruct his crew to go to it. This meant prepare a clambake for the next evening at sundown for his twenty guests.

Nowadays it is every man for himself. However the menu has not really changed since the Republic was formed, nor has the way settlers learned to cook the corn and shellfish in the ad hoc ovens, or pits, invented by the Indians. The New England or Yankee clambake is as much a national feast as is Thanksgiving. And most people have a last glorious binge on the beach at the end of August before they return to the city from their long summer holidays.

The first clambake I attended was in Martha's Vineyard on a lovely beach of dunes capped with long willowy beachgrass. I was told to bring a sweater, although the temperature at 5 p.m. was about 85 degrees. I was given a basket to carry, surprisingly heavy. I found out later that it was full of vodka and gin. We arrived to find a blazing fire and much consternation. It was supposed to have turned to embers by then, but the wind had risen and whipped up the blaze. And the smoke – Oh Lord – had everyone coughing, rubbing their eyes, retreating frantically from the 'bake' pits and yelling for drinks.

Soon we were consoled with large gins in paper cups, and someone kept running the line of teary-eyed spectators offering ice, ice, any-one? And along came a teenager shaking peanuts out of a large bag. Unfortunately, most of them fell to the sand as we swayed in the wind which was becoming stronger and colder. Meanwhile the younger, more durable element had managed to damp down the fire and were endeavouring to place the clams around the blistery sea-weed whose water would cook them.

Hours passed, the moon came up, and the wind changed. We had to turn our backs to the fire and wrap our much-needed sweaters around us, at the same time trying to keep the sand from getting into every nook and cranny of our weather-whipped bodies.

But then came the cry, 'Clams up!' Several young men appeared with plates piled with clams, sweet potatoes, corn, a small lobster, and a large paper napkin. My nearest companion turned to grab a plateful when a gust of wind caught us and everything fell into the sand. 'Don't touch it yet, it's burning hot,' went down the line. So we all had another restorative drink.

Eventually we found a bit of everything, gratiné with sand. What to do? Obviously stagger to the sea, wash the food off quickly in the water, and eat it with our fingers. I tried, goodness knows, I tried! But I remember only getting wet to the thighs as a big wave struck, knocking the plate from my hand. Thank heavens it was dark. As I trudged back, jeans clinging dankly to my thighs, someone said, 'What wonderful clams. Didn't you think the lobster was great?' I replied, 'Yes, absolutely wonderful, never had anything so good, but it sure makes one thirsty.'

At least I had managed to hold onto my cup and received an immediate fill-up. As I neared the fire, I managed to salvage a baked potato from a friendly helper. I was torn between eating it or stashing it behind my knee as one does at an Irish point-to-point. We now crouched wetly in the moonlight. Someone started to sing, 'By the sea, by the beautiful sea,' and I looked around wildly for anyone who might be leaving in a car. At last I spied a landrover driving off, and begged a lift. 'We're full,' they said. 'You'll have to get in the back.' I clambered in, and what did I see but the remains of the clams, buttery corn on the cob, baby lobster, hard rolls and plates of sweet potatoes. Bumping along the potholed road back to the Vine-yard I had the best, and possibly the last, clambake I would ever enjoy.

To Arrange a Clambake

The night before the feast make a small pit of sand and line it with rocks and flat stones. Build a fire and tend it through the day. By night-time the ash should be flat on the rocks. The stones and rocks are by now extremely hot. Then bank the fire and leave it. The next day, early in the morning, make a fire again on top of what is left.

The picnic consists of fresh lobsters, clams, corn cobs wrapped in foil (these used to be wrapped in vine leaves) and sweet potatoes baked in their jackets. Cover the whole thing with seaweed and then put a wet tarpaulin over the top and leave roughly from 9 a.m. until 10 p.m., by which time all should be ready and tender. The seaweed supplies the flavour, keeps the moisture in and steams all the seafood. Now we also add half a broiler chicken, again in layers of seaweed, and this is delicious. People lie in the grass around this non-smoking fire and drink draught beer or cider. It's an all-day event.

About Clambakes

Whatever the size of your bake, dig your clams the day before. Scrub them well to remove sand. Put them in a bucket, well covered with sea water. Add corn meal, allowing ½ cup to 2 quarts water. The cereal helps rid the clams of sand and internal waste. Leave the clams in a cool place. Rinse and drain them just before using.

Clambake
(for 20 people)

200 soft-shell clams	20 1½-lb (700 g) lobsters or
50 hard-shell clams (optional)	5 pecks soft-shell crabs
4 dozen ears of corn	Butter, melted
5 broiling chickens	Beer or cider
10 sweet potatoes	Watermelon
20 frankfurters (optional)	Coffee

Start preparations at least 4 hours before you plan to serve. Dig a sand pit 1 foot deep and 3½ feet across. Line it with smooth round rocks. Be sure the rocks have not been baked before. Have a wet tarpaulin – generous enough to overlap the pit area by 1 foot all round – and a few rocks handy to weight the edges. Build a fire over the rock surface, using hardwood, and keep feeding it for the next 2½ to 3 hours while the rocks are heating. Gather and wash about 4 bushels of wet rock seaweed. In fact, it is wise to soak the seaweed for at least 45 minutes before use. Have a pail of sea water at hand.

Partially husk the ears of corn. Do not pull them quite clean but leave on the last layer or two. Rip these back far enough to remove the silk. Then replace them, so the kernels are fully protected. Reserve the pulled husks.

Quarter the chickens. You may wrap the chicken pieces in cheesecloth or divide the food into 20 individual cheesecloth-wrapped servings, so that each person's food can later be removed as one unit.

Scrub the lobsters or crabs.

Now you are ready to arrange for the 'bake'. Rake the embers from the hot stones, remove them from the pit and line it with the wet seaweed, covering the stones. The lining should be about 6 inches deep. Put over it, if you wish, a piece of chicken wire. If you haven't wrapped the individual servings in cheesecloth, pack the pit in layers. For added flavour, put down first a layer of hard-shell clams, then the frankfurters if you use them, then the lobsters or crabs, the chicken and the soft-shell clams, the sweet potatoes and the ears of corn. You may also put seaweed between the layers. Cover the layered food with the reserved corn husks and sprinkle the whole with the bucket of sea water. Quickly cover with the wet tarpaulin. Weight the tarpaulin down well with rocks. The whole should steam covered for about 1 hour. During the steaming, it will puff up, which is a sign of a satisfactory 'bake'. To test, lift the tarpaulin carefully at one corner so as not to get sand into the pit and see if the clams have opened. If so, the whole feast should be cooked just to the right point. Have handy plenty of towels and melted butter.

Serve with beer or cider, with water-melon and coffee to follow.

A Painter's Picnic

DEREK HILL

Thinking back over picnics is, I find, no strain to my memory: the landscape, to a painter, is as important as the meal itself. I remember picnics in all sorts of places: in pinewoods in Bavaria, dashing down to a nearby lake to bathe with my cousins while my mother and aunt Lucy watched, trying to photograph our splashings with trembling hands and shaky results. Then, a few years later when I was a student, picnics in France during painting excursions under those exquisite Ile de France skies of floating clouds and Impressionist river scenes; rarely attended by French friends, who, when they did overcome their dislike of informality and the deep countryside, insisted on correct *plâcement* and table linen.

In post-war years there was a vividly remembered picnic in Turkey at a Hittite site – an ambassadorial picnic with the chief archaeological experts in the country as our guides. A liveried chauffeur helped with the 'furniture' and the 'site' – custodians stood at a respectful distance watching the unusual scene. We had a delectable cold Turkish soup called leyla that I was greedy enough to get the recipe for.

Sandwiches – in spite of my grandmother having made a dictionary of them in her handwritten book of recipes – are the one thing that I can do without at any meal, unless they are of the delicious and thinly cut cucumber variety that used to be offered at tennis-party teas. Nowadays they are never thin enough, and the cucumber is seldom peeled. But back to my grandmother: she listed sandwiches of chopped figs and lemon cream, dates, bananas, herring with mustard sauce, olives chopped with ham and cheese, sardines and watercress – an infinite and mouth-watering variety. Today the bread always seems too heavy for the filling, and after one mouthful one feels 'full up to dollies' wax', as Nanny used to call one's bloated state.

'If you live, as I do, in one of the wettest climates in the British Isles (Donegal) something warm is needed, and something that can be eaten in a shelter or a neighbour's porch, should the wind and rain be too extreme. It is a rule here never to cancel a picnic because of the weather, which can change completely within a matter of hours. A large thermos filled with risotto or kedgeree is popular, and then a salad packed into a big apple-shaped ice bucket that keeps it cool and fresh; cheese and a tin of Bath Oliver biscuits and slices of almond cake in foil. I am fortunate enough to own a Sardinian wicker basket which kind Italian friends bought me as a house present; it is 'upholstered' inside with all possible picnic requirements and large enough to hold a banquet.

This picnic essay started about landscape as an ingredient essential to a painter's pleasure, but a more culinary and basic interest has inevitably intervened. Perhaps Bernard Berenson was right when he used to say, 'The trouble with Derek is that he never paints between meals.' I know that even on a perfect day in the most beautiful surroundings, I often regret that my Sardinian basket isn't stocked with paints and brushes rather than the splendid provisions packed by Gracie, my housekeeper.

Leyla Soup
(for four)

1 tablespoon butter	1½ lemons
1 heaped dessertspoon flour	1 pint (570 ml) yoghurt
2 pints (1 litre 150 ml) chicken stock	Freshly chopped mint
	2 tablespoons tomato juice
2 eggs	Salt and pepper

Melt the butter and slightly cook the flour in it. Add the stock slowly: bring to the boil, stirring all the time. Beat the eggs till they froth, add the strained juice of the lemons, and stir into the stock (having first added a few tablespoons of the stock to the egg and lemon) very slowly. Bring to the boil again. Add the yoghurt but do not reboil.

Add salt, mint, pepper, etc., and, if liked, tomato juice – fresh if possible. This soup can be consumed hot as well as cold.

Almond Cake

5 oz (150 g) almonds	*Filling*
6 oz (175 g) caster sugar	8 oz (225 g) butter, softened
A few drops of vanilla	8 oz (225 g) icing sugar,
essence	sieved
5 egg whites	2 oz (50 g) melted chocolate
Toasted, chopped almonds	1 teaspoon rum or sherry

Preheat the oven to gas mark 5 (375° F, 190° C). Rub the almonds and sugar together. Add vanilla. Whip the egg whites stiffly and fold into the almond mixture. Using a piping bag, pipe 3 or 4 spiral rounds onto a greased and floured baking sheet and bake for 15 minutes.

Mix the filling ingredients together. Coat the almond rounds with it and pile one on top of the other. Finally spread the top and sides with the filling and sprinkle with toasted, chopped almonds.

Derek Hill.

Charlotte Horsfield, 'A Welsh Picnic' (Charlotte Horsfield)

Hugh Honour, 'A White Picnic'. Left to right: John Fleming and
Hugh Honour (Ian Graham)

Angela Huth: 'The Perfect Picnic'. Sir Frederick and Lady Warner with friends (Angela Huth)

MIDDLE PICTURE· Clara Johnston, 'A Maharaja's Picnic Tea', "The Tent Club at Tiffin" (Percy Carpenter, by courtesy of Eyre and Hobhouse Ltd)
ABOVE· Elizabeth Leicester, 'Holkham Shooting Lunches'. The boy is the late Lord Leicester (husband of Elizabeth Leicester) aged 7

Susanna Johnston,
'February Picnic in Cadaquez'
Nicholas Johnston and José
(Susanna Johnston)

Roddy Llewellyn,
'Picnic at the Glen' (Anne Tennant)

Rupert Loewenstein, 'Caldo e Cremoso', ▷
Rupert and Josephine Loewenstein
and Countess Foscari

Patrick Lindsay, 'Fourth of June Picnic'. Left to right: Colin and Alan
Clark, Lady Crawford, Lady Clark, Lord Clark, Lord Crawford
and Patrick Lindsay (Lent by Derek Hill)

The
McGillycuddy
of the Reeks,
'An Irish Picnic'
Richard
with sister and
parents

Gregory Martin,
'Picnic Command'
(Carey Basset)
▽

Mark Maufe,
'A Boating Picnic
in Overy Staithe'
The Maufe family
(Anne Tennant)

HRH The
Princess Margaret,
'Picnic at Hampton
Court'

Margaret Vyner, ▷
'Dominican Picnic'

Gaia Servadio, 'The
Kingdom of Picnics'.
Right: Gaia Servadio
and her daughter
Allegra
▽

Colin Tennant, 'Mustique' (Patrick Lichfield)

John Julius Norwich,
'Sahara Picnics'

Freya Stark, 'Dartmoor Picnic'
(Charles Harding)

Francis Watson, 'A Picnic in the Grand Manner' (Orford Town Trust)

William Weaver, 'A Spontini Picnic'
(Susanna Johnston)

Anne Tennant,
'Preparations for a
Shooting Picnic at
Holkham'

Tanya Vinogradoff, 'A Dorsetshire Picnic'
(Tanya Vinogradoff)

Autumn Mushroom Picnic

MIN HOGG

If you cannot tell the difference between edible types of wild mushroom and their dangerously poisonous counterparts, this picnic plan could be the most effective way of pruning your circle of friends since dinner at the Borgias. All the same, if you cannot distinguish between them you are missing one of the most delicious of gastronomic treats. I urge you from the bottom of my heart to rectify the situation. Just check on the cost of wild mushrooms in the shops, should you be lucky enough to know of a greengrocer with the enterprise to sell them. It will be enough to convince the profoundest sceptic that they must not only be a delicacy worth trying, but also be worth the price of a guidebook on mushrooms and fungi in order to learn how to obtain the treat for free. There are masses of guides to wild mushrooms in bookshops, and one I find particularly easy to use is called *British and European Mushrooms and Fungi*, published by Chatto and Windus. It is cheap, pocket-size, and every photograph is in colour. The mixture of stern warnings and bubbling enthusiasm in its text seems like a good balance, and it certainly gave me the confidence right from the start to identify and eat what I had picked.

One pale blue morning in mid-October I gathered a basket of mixed mushrooms. They came from a Hampshire woodland spot I know, within sight and sound of the M3. You would be amazed how many rich clusters of fungi are to be found in woods close beside motorways.

Since so many lethal-looking toadstools, are, in fact, edible, it is vital to educate yourself about those that have the best taste. There are lots that are either insipid or repulsively slimy, and I have never generated much enthusiasm amongst my guests for anything blue – these are the sort to leave gracing the paths and glades in which they grow. Beginners in toadstool eating should really confine themselves to the Cep and Boletus families; they are delicious and abundant and have the distinguishing feature of something looking like fine sponge rubber on their undersides in place of the gills found in ordinary shop-bought mushrooms. Incidentally I advise scraping off this benign but slippery sponge stuff before cooking, rather in the way you remove the hairy bit attached to artichoke hearts. Apart from the guidebook, essential at all times, pickers should arm themselves with a knife to slice off the mushroom caps; wrenching the whole stem out of the ground stops other mushrooms from coming up in the same place.

While I was foraging for this picnic my guests were working like Trojans collecting wood and building a really good fire at our chosen site beside a lake. We balanced over the fire a metal trivet large enough to take two pans: one pan for water – which I had brought as hot as possible in giant thermoses – and the other for the mushrooms. Since the fungi taste extremely rich I decided to cook them as they often do in Italy, sliced and sautéed with parsley and garlic to flavour a simple pasta. As we waited for the spaghetti water to boil I sliced the mushrooms, mixed them with the chopped parsley and crushed garlic, and fried them gently in a little butter. The best spaghetti for picnics is vermicelli. I like its thin gauge which has the inestimable advantage of cooking quickly – even on an open fire.

The minute the pasta was *al dente* and drained, I tipped the mushrooms together with the pan juices on top of it, mixed them all together, and dished them up as quickly as possible.

Min Hogg

A White Picnic

HUGH HONOUR

My ideal of a perfect picnic belongs to the 1950s, not later or earlier. Childhood treats were all very well in a Betjemanesque way. I too 'used to picnic where the thrift/grew deep and tufted to the edge'. But today, driving along the Autoroute south of Lyon, I read the signs *'Pique-nique jeux d'enfants'* as a warning rather than an invitation – though the phrase does have a ring of Verlaine about it. Most of my picnics nowadays are eaten on journeys across Europe by road. The company, limited to a maximum of four, is always that of old friends. The food, bought in the town where we spent the previous night, is also well-tried – in Italy cold roast sucking pig and the best baked bread to be found anywhere in Europe now (much better than in France where it used to be so delicious), in Spain strongly flavoured ham, in Germany liver sausage, in France a selection of pâtés and galantines and *oeufs en gêlée*. These picnics are no more than brief affairs, however, intervals in a long drive, and never quite match up to my or any other ideal. The *oeufs en gêlée* too often prove to be hard-boiled, not *mollets*. The place where we stop attracts others almost immediately, and seldom seems in retrospect as congenial as the one we had passed only a few minutes earlier or the one we noticed soon afterwards.

For me the perfect picnic must be incidental, just part of a journey through country beautiful in itself and, if possible, with literary or historical associations as well. My ideal picnic began to form twenty-five years or so ago when I lived in Percy Lubbock's villa, Gli Scafari, near Lerici – a house of cool marmorial beauty perched on a rocky promontory above the crystalline blue of the still unpolluted Mediterranean, with a wide view of distant islands and the little fishing village of Porto Venere on the northern arm of the Gulf of La Spezia. The air was drowsy with literary associations. Percy himself had been at Cambridge with E. M. Forster – 'poor old Morgan,' as he often remarked, 'he never knew quite the "right" people.' Later he had been a disciple of Henry James, whose voice and conversation he could mimic when well-primed after dinner, and, for a time, one of Edith Wharton's 'young men' – though he was banished from her little court when he married another wealthy cosmopolitan blue-stocking. Only a few hundred yards away D. H. Lawrence had spent the winter of 1913–14 in a four-room pink cottage on the shore of 'a little tiny bay half shut in by rocks, and smothered by olive woods that slope down swiftly'. Beneath Gli Scafari there was a huge, arching grotto, one of those, we liked to think, that Shelley had explored by boat during the last weeks of his life when he lived at San Terenzo on the other side of Lerici. Byron, on his way from Pisa to Genoa in October 1823, stopped at Lerici for a few nights and made himself ill by swimming far out to sea with Trelawny and eating a large dinner while treading water – one of the most bizarre picnics on record. Next year he was to sail along the same coast on his last voyage, to Missolonghi. But, as we watched from the loggia the passage of shipping out at sea or making for harbour at La Spezia or Porto Venere, there was another figure from the past who haunted our imaginations – Walter Pater.

I had first read *Marius the Epicurean* at school and thought it, as did the young Max Beerbohm, a marvellous 'tale of adventure, quite as fascinating as *Midshipman Easy*, and far less hard to understand because there were no nautical terms in it'. At Lerici I found myself near Marius's country. His villa, White Nights, was among the hills a few miles inland. Pater wrote that 'the traveller, descending from the slopes of Luna even as he got his first view of the "Port-of-Venus" would pause by the way, to read the face, as it were, of so beautiful a dwelling-place, lying away from the white road, at the point where it began to descend somewhat steeply to the marsh-land below'. Each of the windows of Marius's tower chamber framed a landscape, 'the pallid crags of Carrara, like wildly twisted snow-drifts above the purple heath; the distant harbour with its freight of white marble going to sea; the lighthouse temple of "Venus Speciosa" on its dark headland, amid the long-drawn curves of white breakers'. The description is circumstantial enough to suggest that Pater, who could have passed this way when he went to Pisa, had a particular spot in mind. To find it became the object of many excursions and picnics.

Near the little village of Fosdinovo there are several places which almost match Pater's description. From there one can see the Carrara mountains, uncannily like those in the background to the *Mona Lisa* which inspired one of Pater's over-familiar purple passages. Glimpses may be caught of an ancient amphitheatre among vineyards, all that remains above ground of the city of Luni from which Carrara marble was exported throughout the Roman Empire. But to find a point from which Porto Venere can also be seen is difficult. I never succeeded in locating it. If found, this would be the place for the perfect, the truly Epicurean picnic.

Special food would, of course, be eaten, food of a preciosity to suit the occasion and predominantly white. We should begin with fish, cold fillets of sole or shelled scampi and a very pale mayonnaise. Then there might be chicken breasts or quails, stuffed with white truffles and wrapped in the most delicately streaked bacon, lightly fried, accompanied by a white salad such as is sometimes served in Italy in early spring – raw fennel cut into little strips, celery, chicory and paper-thin flakes of turnip sprinkled over with violet flowers to delight both eye and palate. To end we should have a cheese mousse of the type the cook at Gli Scafari used to prepare, firm yet crumbly to the fork and wonderfully light, composed mainly of ricotta (ewe's milk cheese) but according to a recipe I have never been able to trace. We should drink a dry white wine, Verdicchio from the Marche. And afterwards, until the sun sinks into the sea, we would read Pater's 'oft-read tale' again, from the edition printed on hand-made paper with title page designed by Herbert Horne, the biographer of Botticelli and one of the last Anglo-Italians of whom Pater might have wholly approved. But the place has not been, and may never be, found. So my perfect picnic remains an untarnished ideal – forever cold and still to be enjoyed.

Hugh Honour.

A Welsh Picnic

CHARLOTTE HORSFIELD

Welsh picnics fall into one or other of two categories: the premeditated and the unpremeditated. Much planning will go into the premeditated picnic, particularly when several families are involved, with Ordnance Survey maps being spread out in a number of households and map references being agreed over the telephone. Vehicles with four-wheel drive will be commissioned to bring to the site equipment, the old, the very young, or the less vigorous members of the party. The picnic fare on such an occasion requires forward planning. I am indebted to a friend who has perfected the art of picnicking for the following recipe.

Lamb Kebabs

1 leg of lamb	Black pepper
1 bottle red wine	Salt
½ pint (275 ml) olive oil	1 lb (450 g) firm tomatoes
1 onion, roughly chopped	2–3 green peppers
2–3 cloves garlic, chopped	Several onions

On the day before the picnic you buy the leg of lamb. You take it home and set to work on it, cutting it up into 1 inch (2.5 cm) pieces, having first removed all fat and sinew. You then make a marinade by mixing together the red wine, olive oil, garlic, black pepper and salt. Leave the meat in this marinade for about 24 hours.

On the day of the picnic chop the tomatoes into pieces and add the juice and the pips to the marinade. Cut the green peppers and onions into pieces about 1 inch (2.5 cm) square.

A certain amount of hardware must then be assembled for cooking the kebabs at the picnic. You will need a portable barbecue. If no such thing is readily available it can be constructed from a biscuit tin which will need to have holes bored in its base for ventilation. You will then need four half-bricks on which to stand the tin, charcoal for fuel, firelighters and matches with which to ignite it, and a pair of bellows to encourage the glowing charcoals. You should also take a couple of cake racks to lay across the biscuit tin once the firelighters have burnt away and the charcoal is hot. Nor must you forget the skewers onto which pieces of meat, green pepper and onion are threaded alternatively before being placed across the heat for a thorough cooking. Bring with you some oven gloves so that the pleasure of the day is not marred by burnt fingers. If an advance party can reach the picnic spot a little early so that the cooking can be started by the time the main body of walkers arrive with appetites that have been stimulated in fresh mountain air, this recipe can be guaranteed to please.

Wholemeal Buns

½ oz (10 g) fresh yeast
½ pint (275 ml) warm water
1 dessertspoon black
  treacle or molasses
1 lb (450 g) wholemeal
  flour
1 tablespoon olive oil
1 teaspoon sea salt

Place the yeast in a large mixing bowl. Pour onto it the warm water mixed with black treacle or molasses. Stir until the yeast has dissolved and then add some of the flour until you have a batter. Leave to rise in a warm place for about 20 minutes or until it begins to froth. Add salt, olive oil and the rest of the flour. Knead the dough for about 5 minutes. Return to the bowl and leave in a warm spot for about an hour, by which time it should have doubled in size. Once more turn the dough onto the floured board and knead.

Now divide the dough into twelve and knead each roll until it is smooth. Shape the rolls, either round or oblong, and lay them side by side with spaces in between in a large greased baking tin. Put in a

104 The Picnic Papers

warm place and again leave to prove until they have doubled in size. This may take 30–40 minutes. Preheat the oven to gas mark 6 (400° F, 200° C).

Bake for 30–35 minutes. Turn out on to a wire cake rack until cool. The whole process takes about three hours.

Charlotte Horsfield

The Perfect Picnic

ANGELA HUTH

There are picnics of the mind and picnics in real life. Most people have experienced both and know the difference between them.

In the imagination the *déjeuners sur l'herbe* which we attend seem to be very similar. There is always warmth, but cool shade, iced white wine, grass that doesn't prickle, butterflies – a veritable impressionist picture, happily out of focus. If the imagination were unkind enough to look closer, the dream would be broken.

In reality the dream is broken, almost inevitably, as soon as the very idea of a picnic is cast abroad, and the hamper packed. (Hamper indeed: where are the hampers of yesteryear, those magnificent whicker baskets, lids slotted with knives and forks, and stacked with their special plates? It is supermarket plastic bags in which we pack our feasts of today, and they are not at all the same.)

But disillusionment is of no matter to the determined picnicker. Once launched on the expedition, he blooms with optimism however black the cloud that billows from nowhere, however large the spots of rain. On, on he drives past those Picnic Areas whose corrugated lavatories and official rustic tables make him sad to think this generation of townsfolk think *they* are proper picnic places. On to a small stretch of balding coast with a misted view over a grim sea. The wind might die down, but until it does where better to eat than the stuffy cosiness of the car, thick with the smells of melons, cheese and wet dogs? Children shriek, there's strawberry jam on the steering wheel and, by heavens, it's almost the fun we had imagined.

For there is probably no hardier race of picnickers than the

British. On Bodmin Moor I have watched summer sleet sizzle the flames of the barbecue on which lie dozens of drenched *langoustines*, where in a nearby bowl *fraises du bois* turn to pulp. But the smiles of the crowd gathered under their anoraks wavered not. I have seen members of the edge-of-the-motorway brigade sprayed black with mud by passing cars as they enjoy their sliced-bread sandwiches. I have seen train spotters relishing Chinese takeaways on a stack of mailbags at Paddington Station on a November afternoon.

But happily, whatever the disappointment of real-life picnics, in retrospect it is the delights that are remembered. And thus our nostalgia for picnics. We continue to persevere with them, for when they work they are occasions of particular pleasure.

My own first memories of picnic life were at the age of twelve: curried egg sandwiches at sunless Overstrand. My sister and I – elasticated bathing suits and gooseflesh thighs – sat on a tartan rug scoffing at our parents' tweed coats and mackintoshes. Eight years later there were picnic lunches at point-to-points in Hampshire – occasions of supreme sophistication, those. The backs of Land Rovers were let down to reveal the last of the real hampers of delicious food. I don't remember precisely *what* food. I have no recollection of quiches in those mid-fifties days – they were to become fashionable much later. But I do remember sturdy wicker baskets with separate compartments for bottles of drink: and standing round with tiny glasses in fuzzy-gloved hands, sipping cherry brandy and sloe gin against the cold.

The point of those picnics was not, of course, the food (or even the horses) but the chance to brush against the fancied member of the Bullingdon Club and be offered a sausage on a stick with a look of such penetrating desire that the legs would tremble in the gumboots like grass in a wind. How beautiful they were, those sporting young men in their riding macs that clacked like a field of cabbages when they moved – their greenish trilbies cocked saucily over one eye, their incredible eyelashes, and small patches of mysteriously long hair on their cheeks. No wonder the contents of the hampers were of no consequence.

But of all memorable picnics the one nearest to perfection of imaginary picnics took place in Cornwall four years ago. It was the inspiration of those master picnickers, Marika and Robin Hanbury-Tenison. She was one of our finest cooks. He is a renowned explorer. They have feasted off rattlesnakes and spiders in many a foreign jungle in their time, but at home on Bodmin Moor their picnics were incomparable.

It was May, very warm. We were asked to wear Edwardian clothes, and to meet in the bluebell woods. These woods were sprawled about along a valley – crumbling old trees, lichen-covered – their frizz of new leaves a-dazzle with spring sun. Our chosen place was on the mossy banks of a stream: a place where wild thyme grew. Tables were laid with damask cloths, and spread with a feast in keeping with the Edwardian era. We lay on cashmere rugs, crushing bluebells. We ate iced strawberry soup, chicken and bacon pie, cherries in wine and pyramids of meringues. Suddenly through the trees came our elegant Ambassador to Japan, Sir Fred Warner. He wore a blazer, straw boater and almond-pink silk tie. Behind him rustled his wife, Simone, in forget-me-not blue, who sang to us in her clear piping voice while her small sons fell in and out of the stream. There will never be another picnic like that middle-aged frolic in the bluebell woods, but there will be others of surprising and enchanting character, and in old age we perennial picnickers will still be there, sharing the present delight beneath umbrella or parasol, remembering all the while the hampers of our youth.

Strawberry Soup

2 chicken stock cubes	Salt, pepper
1 pint (570 ml) water	½ teaspoon ground ginger
2 lb (900 g) fresh or	1 small carton natural yoghurt
frozen strawberries	2 tablespoons finely
½ teaspoon mixed herbs	chopped chives

Combine the chicken stock cubes and water, bring to the boil and stir until the cubes are dissolved. Add the strawberries and herbs, season with salt and pepper, and mix in the ground ginger. Bring to the boil, simmer for 5 minutes and then rub through a fine sieve to remove the seeds. Stir in the yoghurt, mix until smooth, and serve hot or iced with a garnish of chopped chives.

A Pyrenean Picnic

MILES JEBB

Since mountaineers are usually obliged to carry all their own provisions, their picnics all too often consist only of spartan snacks hardly qualifying for mention in this book – hard-boiled eggs, tomatoes, chocolate, fruit and suchlike. But a mountaineering or walking expedition need not always be a gastronomic non-event, and if it can be arranged around an al fresco lunch it is miraculously converted from a masochistic ordeal into an epicurean indulgence: and how much better all food tastes when one is tired and hungry!

A notable instance of this obvious truth was a picnic in the Basque Pyrenees, high up on a ridge straddling the Franco–Spanish border. An essential element of the art of the picnic must be the selection of the site, and this one was quite remarkable. Shaded from the hot July sun at the upper edge of a forest of scrub oaks, we sat on stones and gazed down into the deep valleys whose tumbling streams provide the headwaters of the river Bidassoa, splendidly isolated from the rest of humanity by hours of mountain walking. A party of discerning French friends clearly expected and required a picnic worthy of the setting, and this indeed is what we now enjoyed, once we had got a bonfire crackling beneath a face of rock.

An immense frying pan which had been tantalisingly suspended from the backpack of the strongest of the party now came into use for the preparation of that famous Basque dish, piperade. Piperade may be described as halfway between scrambled eggs and a Spanish omelette; and of all egg dishes this is the one I most recommend for similar picnics, even if they are far removed from the Pyrenees.

For a picnic the peppers can be cut and scraped and the tomatoes skinned beforehand, and carried in a jar; so that all that is needed is to start frying the onion, and after it has softened to add the peppers and tomatoes. As for the eggs, they can simply be dropped into the pan, then stirred to scramble. Piperade should be accompanied by thin slices of jambon de Bayonne or prosciutto.

Such was our Pyrenean picnic, eaten off paper plates with plastic forks. It was followed by goats' cheese and fruit, and was accompanied by a beaker of Bordeaux – though for thirst-quenching we had lots of plastic bottles of Evian. Finally, coffee was brewed in a saucepan: good, strong, French coffee; and with it a mountaineer's liqueur – a lump of sugar soaked in Armagnac, at once sustaining energy and inducing a state of happy disregard of aching limbs. I must not forget to mention that the meal was very nearly missed for lack of a light for the bonfire (eventually obtained from a passer-by) so in this non-smoking age don't forget matches as you prepare for your picnic.

Miles Jebb

A Maharaja's Picnic Tea

CLARA JOHNSTON

One afternoon when nothing much was happening in the City Palace, Bubbles, the Maharaja of Jaipur, decided to take us to see his father's old shooting lodge about fifteen miles outside Jaipur. A picnic was prepared and put into the back of the American jeep along with Clare Steel, the uniformed bodyguard and myself.

In Jaipur, Bubbles is still thought of as the king and those who recognized the T-shirted driver clasped their hands together and bowed as we drove by.

Across a plain, along a thin, straight road, we passed ox-drawn carts brimming with hay and people and stopped for a moment at a lake which stretched for miles without so much as a ripple on its polished surface.

Later the land became hillier and the vegetation more dense. Just before we reached a great dam, Bubbles turned down a driveway lined with rambling shrubs. At the gate two octogenerian servants tumbled down the steps to greet us, as if our arrival had awoken them from a deep sleep.

The house had not been visited for some time and smelled of dust and mothballs. Built in the thirties, it looked like an Italian villa with pastel yellow stuccoed walls, balconies, shuttered windows and a loggia. The house had been used as a shooting lodge for the surrounding area and the hall was lined with stuffed tigers, bears and lions.

Below the front of the house was a stone hideout with square peep holes. Years ago the sport was to tie a bull to the hideout and wait for a tiger to approach. Those who were brave enough watched the event from within while the rest watched safely from the house.

We sat, unthreatened by tigers, in the garden and the aged servants spread a white linen tablecloth over a round wooden table in the centre of the lawn. The picnic, a mixture of traditional English sandwiches and Indian spices, was spread out on the table by the bodyguard: cucumber sandwiches, spiced chicken, poppadums, curd raitas and sweets. We drank tea out of a thermos – a picnic item inherited from the English – and watched the sun set over the lake.

Curd (Yoghurt) Raitas

1 pint (450 ml) plain yoghurt
Juice of half a lemon
2 cloves of garlic (crushed)
Chopped mint leaves
Finely chopped fresh green chilli

Pour yoghurt into a bowl and beat in the rest of the ingredients.

For variations you can add to taste: 1 teaspoon paprika, a pinch of cayenne, a pinch of coriander, coriander leaves or a pinch of cumin. Other ingredients such as raisins, sultanas, sliced bananas, grated carrots, chopped nuts or diced boiled new potatoes can be added. You can make it into a salad by adding raw vegetables.

Poppadums

Some of the ingredients for poppadums are not available in England so I have adapted it slightly.

3–4 tablespoons flour
Salt
Carraway seeds
A little red pepper
Cream or milk

Season the flour with salt and add carraway seeds and red pepper. Mix with cream or milk to a stiff paste. Knead well, roll out a little, cut into cubes of 1–1½ inches diameter. Take each cube, roll it and fold it and roll it again, finally beating it with a rolling pin until it is paper-thin and the size of a side plate. Prick each slice all over with a fork, lay on a greased and floured baking sheet and bake for three minutes or so in a very hot oven. The poppadums should blister and be very thin and crisp.

Clara Johnston

February Picnic in Cadaquez

SUSANNA JOHNSTON

Be sure to be armed with a glove and strong pair of scissors to open *garotas* – Catalan for sea urchin – straight from the sea in February. We were promised these several days running, but each day the sea was too rough for the fishermen. At last the conditions were right and we lugged a huge cardboard boxful to San Sebastian – an erstwhile hermitage on top of the highest mountain above Cadaquez, which you reach by winding and wrenching the car up a twisting road which, from above, looks like a strangled intestine spreading over the mountain.

You cut the urchins in two and empty out the liquid surrounding the pink roes. Clean out all the slimy black muck and sprinkle with lemon and black pepper. Scoop out the edible bit with circles of fresh bread and pop them into your mouth. Though hardly filling, they are undeniably nourishing, and strongly fish-flavoured. After this good tuck-in we settled ourselves on a sunny rock looking down onto the harbour four miles below, and started on the more substantial dishes: anchovy butter, pig's liver pâté, oranges and apples and a hot *tisane* made from a variety of dried herbs which grow on the hill where we sat. When the sun disappeared, quite suddenly, we remembered that it was still February and retreated to the hermitage for coffee and liqueurs.

Anchovy Butter

Quantitites of these ingredients depend on taste and numbers:

Cream cheese   Pounded anchovy
Grated capers   fillets
Grated onions   Thick cream

Mash all the above together with enough cream to produce a good spreadable consistency.

Susanna Johnston.

Picnic at Bagni di Lucca

SUSANNA JOHNSTON

We drove along the Valley of the Serchio which lies between the Apennines and the Appian Alps towards Bagni di Lucca, a little spa beloved by English poets and writers throughout the centuries for its warm sulphur baths and for being permanently shaded by overhanging mountains and thick chestnut woods. We were making for the small Protestant cemetery where Ouida (the novelist Louise de la Ramée, who took her own childish mispronunciation of her first name as her nom-de-plume) lies buried. This cemetery is not easy to storm, and bribery and negotiation with the neighbours is needed.

Ouida died of pneumonia in the severe winter of 1909 at the age of sixty-nine; and was buried at Bagni di Lucca after years of degradation and near-blindness, deserted by all but her faithful dog. The English consul of the time is said to have been moved by her bleak end and to have paid for her beautiful tomb in the style of the Della Quercia effigy of 1406 in the Duomo at Lucca. By the time we met our friends at the pretty iron gateway to the cemetery the Tuscan heavens had opened. We pulled our coats over our heads, covered our baskets as best we could, and belted up the path to a small deserted chapel which, to our delight, turned out to be used for storing bales of hay. These we quickly rearranged to provide ourselves with table and benches – using rugs as a tablecloth. In no time we were very snug, looking out at a drenched Ouida and the overhanging mountains half-hidden in mist and beating rain. Surrounded as we were by chestnut woods, it seemed appropriate to start with this soup, kept hot in a large thermos.

Chestnut Soup or *Zuppa di Castagne*

1 lb (450 g) chestnuts   2 oz (50 g) butter
2 onions, chopped   Salt
2 carrots, sliced   Pepper
1 piece celery   Stock

Score the chestnuts on their rounded side and bake in a slow oven for 10 minutes. Peel while still warm. In the butter brown the chopped onions, carrots and celery. Add the chestnuts, stock and seasoning. Cook for about 40 minutes until the chestnuts are completely tender and have started to break up. Put the soup through a sieve. Reheat and pour into large thermos.

Chocolate Truffles or *Tartuffi di Cioccolata*

1½ lb (700 g) bitter   2 oz (50 g) butter
  chocolate   1 egg yolk
1 teaspoon milk   1 oz (25 g) cocoa

Melt the chocolate and milk in a double boiler. When smooth take it off the heat and work in the butter and egg yolk. Leave the mixture for 4 or 5 hours. Form into walnut shapes and coat with cocoa powder. These must be eaten within 4 hours and kept very cool. One tablespoon coffee powder can be added to vary the flavour when melting the chocolate.

Susanna Johnston.

I Loathe Picnics

JAMES LEES-MILNE

I loathe picnics.

It may be hereditary. My parents also loathed them as much as they disliked each other, and certainly as much as they disliked us. By some inexplicable mischance it became an established family custom that on the birthday of my sister, my brother and myself the five of us went in a hired punt and one canoe on the River Avon for a picnic. To make matters worse we three children were all born in August. So too was my mother, but I think that only one year did we go on four of these ghastly expeditions in this ill-fated month.

We embarked at Evesham and sailed (if that is the right word) in deadly silence either up- or downstream. If we started downstream there was the impending horror of having to battle against the current on the way back. If we started upstream there was the weir, which meant dragging or carrying the boats several yards overland and the certainty of one of us losing his or her temper. Now the extraordinary thing was that in those distant days when summers were summers and the sun shone from morn till eve it always rained on our birthdays, not intermittently, but consistently, heavily and often catastrophically. Of course we knew beforehand that this would be the case. Nonetheless we went because our parents supposed that we children enjoyed the outings, and that they must dutifully subordinate their strong disinclination to our pleasure. It was only when we were grown up that we dared admit how much we had disliked these expeditions. Our parents groaned. 'If only,' my mother said, 'you had told us so when the eldest of you was five.'

In retrospect these countless picnics merge into one because almost invariably they followed the same pattern and the same proceedings repeated themselves. First there was the unloading of basket, rugs, cushions, sunshades, umbrellas, waterproofs and dogs from car to punt and canoe. Next, the embarrassing scene of my father bargaining with the boatman about the charge, which, if I remember rightly, was thirty shillings for the first three hours and five shillings for each subsequent quarter of an hour. This calculation enraged my father who refused to understand why, were we to spend four hours on the river, the last should cost him a whole pound.

'But you might not come back,' the saucy boatman once dared to remonstrate.

'Do you suppose,' my father replied, drawing himself up to his full six foot two and half inches, 'that I would want to go off with your beastly canoe, leaving you with my new Minerva four-seater? Think again, my good man. Besides, don't you know who I am?' Who was he, anyway?

If we started upstream my mother, who insisted upon having the canoe to herself and the dogs, in spite of my father's warnings, invariably got caught in a whirlpool. She would go round and round and round, desperately paddling in one direction, for she could not reverse, until the bull terrier and the pekineses, made giddy by these gyrations, would jump overboard. This meant that my mother (whose raffia hat had already been knocked off by an overhanging branch) capsized before her madly rotating canoe reached the bank. My father, cursing and swearing 'I told you so', would stretch out the punt pole, exhorting her to grasp it while he towed her ashore. His propulsion of the punt, with the struggling body of his wife at the end of it, was an exceedingly awkward operation for him and an uncomfortable experience for her. At least her immersion settled the vexed question of where to *have* the picnic. If she hadn't fallen in we would have spent ages looking for the right landing place, the right amount of shade (should a ray of sun come out), and the right amount of protection from the inevitable thunderstorm. As it happened, we were obliged to picnic on the sewage farm, next to the gasometer and just beyond the railway siding.

Before we unloaded the picnic basket and other paraphernalia my mother was obliged to strip to the skin, clean off the stinking mud with tufts of rushes and then be wrapped, shivering, with those rugs on which, had the accident not occurred, we would have sat. Thus she squatted like some Egyptian mummy under an igloo of umbrellas. By now my father was in a filthy temper. He, who was by nature a very practical man, refused to do anything but read the *Morning Post* (always a bad sign) which he was obliged to do standing up. He left us children to unpack the basket and spread the paper plates and food on the soggy ground (every rug and mackintosh enveloping my mother). The smell of sewage, gas and my mother was very unappetizing.

Reclining on one elbow with nothing to lean against, even when not eating and drinking with the free hand, has always been torture to me. Besides, the sewage farm did not provide grass, but cinders, if I remember correctly, over which there passed at regular intervals a long, revolving arm which sprayed disinfectant. Memory tells me too that there was seldom enough to eat on our picnics. It never occurred to my mother to tell the cook what food we needed. It was left to the cook to supply chunks of bread and dripping (which children in those days were supposed to like), fids of salty gammon, a few unripe plums and, of course, the birthday cake. On this occasion the bull terrior had sat on the cake, which thereby became a total washout. There would be cider (a great treat) to drink, but not the delicious sweet sort out of a bottle, rather our own home-brewed, bitter sort, unclear and cloudy like some unwholesome liquid from a specimen bottle. There were never enough mugs, and we had to share. I have always had a horror of sharing mugs and would show my disgust. This enraged my father who thought it frightfully cissy. 'Effeminate' was the word he used. Besides, the cider, heady stuff, attracted all the wasps in the Vale of Evesham, as well as little black flies which could not be extracted and had to be swallowed.

After this disgusting and inadequate meal we children had to pack up. We could not take home the remains and my mother – quite rightly – had a horror of litter. We were not allowed to throw the paper in the river, not even the plum stones in case a fish might swallow one and choke. We had to dig a hole with our fingers. Then we had to count the knives, forks and spoons. There was always one missing. From behind the *Morning Post* my father would growl, 'We are not leaving until you have found it.' When it was found my father would put down the paper and yawn. My mother's teeth would chatter. My father would remember an appointment with a man about a horse. He had to get home at once.

We would re-embark. There would be a row among the children about which of us was going to have the canoe because 'shooting the rapids' was the only enjoyable part of the expedition. I, being the most selfish and determined, usually won. Wet, cold, cross and under-nourished, we returned to the boathouse. Looking at his watch, my father would rejoice that we had been on the river for exactly two hours and fifty-five minutes.

How I loathe picnics.

James Lees-Milne

Holkham Shooting Lunches

ELIZABETH LEICESTER

Holkham shooting lunches in the 1920s were spartan, to say the least. The Lord Leicester of the day was so keen on the sport that eating was considered a great waste of time. I remember in the early 1930s one Christmas in deep snow, going out to find the trestle table in a wood. On it were a loaf of bread, a rather hollow Stilton and the famous box of small, raw Spanish onions – a Holkham tradition even today. Their strength cannot be exaggerated; there was not a dry eye round the table and a great deal of nose-blowing went on. The eagerly awaited moment produced a small glass of port which brought some life back into frozen hands and feet.

In later years there were great improvements – lunch indoors with soup, Irish stew and treacle tart kept hot round a blazing fire, with a welcoming drink for each guest.

But the most unusual Holkham dish is velvet. There is a herd of deer in Holkham Park. In the autumn the stags shed a thick skin from their antlers which is collected, fried and served on toast. This delicacy is known as velvet, and was much prized by Lord Leicester who ate it as a savoury. Once at a dinner party we ladies proceeded to the great North Dining-room in full evening dress and wearing long kid gloves, each on the arm of a gentleman in white tie and tails. My partner was very old, nearly blind and deaf. The first course was cockles. Being under-cooked, their shells hadn't opened, so had to be speared with a fork until one gave up with badly bleeding fingers. Sucking pig, then on to the velvet, while a loud and spirited explanation of its origin went on as it congealed on the plate. My neighbour was as hungry at the end of the meal as he had been at the beginning!

Vegetable Pie
(for four approximately)

This superb dish I have never seen in any recipe book or eaten outside our family circle, so, if you get it right, you are in for a real treat! We have never used weights and measures for this pie, so I hope the directions below will prove a success the first time.

6 medium-sized
 potatoes, cooked
2–3 medium onions, sliced
 and lightly fried
2–3 hard-boiled eggs, sliced
3 tomatoes, sliced

4 cupfuls cooked spaghetti
 broken into 3-inch lengths
1 pint béchamel sauce
Salt
Pepper
Butter

In a deep pie dish arrange a layer of sliced potatoes, sprinkle on some of the fried onion, slices of egg, tomatoes, and spaghetti. Pour a generous quantity of béchamel over and season with salt and pepper. Continue this layering, ending with potatoes. Dot with butter and put in medium oven for 15–20 minutes. Finish off under the grill until potatoes are brown.

It is important to have plenty of sauce. This can have different flavourings. One that is excellent is 1 cup of tomato sauce, ½ teaspoon mixed spice and half a dried chilli stirred into the béchamel.

Elizabeth Leicester

The Dales of Moldavia

PATRICK LEIGH FERMOR

It may be rash to intrude this Rumanian feast where so many literary cornucopias are pouring their bounty; for it is the day and the occasion that single out this one, and shadow steals over substance here and veils every memory of what there actually was to eat. (We had set out to pick mushrooms, but they were for dinner.)

The picnic baskets may have contained all sorts of Moldowalkechian wonders – *sarmali* wrapped in vine leaves, fragrant *mititei*, chicken croquettes as light as feathers, a *sterlet* from the Pruth, perhaps, or even, and by the ladleful, wonderful Black Sea caviar from Vâlcov in the Danube delta, on the fringes of Bessarabia; turkey in aspic, almost certainly. Apart from fine indigenous cooking this country seemed to be the meeting place of all that was most delicious in old Russia, Poland, Hungary, Mitteleuropa, France, the Balkans and the Levant. The picnic would have been more likely to start with fierce Moldavian *raki* than with a milder southern *tzuica* of distilled plums; excellent white and red wines, stored in tortuous catacombs, would have accompanied it throughout.

The point of departure was an old and many-legended Cantacuzene country house with inhabitants of indescribable charm. It lay at the heart of a once large but now much reduced estate in High Moldavia, and the time was September 1939. Apart from the two sisters who were our hostesses and their family, there was also, for the summer, Prince Matila Ghyka and three other young English people. (I had become a sort of fixture.) Matila Ghyka, traveller, diplomat, well-known writer on aesthetics – *Le Nombre d'Or, Sortilèges du Verbe*, etc. – and a gastronome famous for his encyclopaedic approach to life, would certainly have had a hand in the planning.

It was a summer of unparalleled beauty and remoteness, but the months passed too fast; the crops were in and the storks were gathering before heading south; and suddenly, not unannounced, the evil omens had begun to multiply quickly, until all seemed black. To forget and exorcise for a day the growing assembly of trouble we set off, on 2 September, to pick those mushrooms in a wood about ten miles away, some of us in an old open carriage, some on horseback; through the vineyards where the grapes were almost ready to be harvested and pressed, and out into the open country. The clearings in the wood, when we arrived, were studded with our quarry. Alighting and dismounting, we scattered in a competitive frenzy, reassembling soon with our baskets full to the brim. In the glade of this mysterious wood, with the tethered horses grazing and swishing their tails under the oak branches, the picnic spun itself out. Soon it was late afternoon and all the bottles were empty and the old Polish coachman was fidgeting the horses back into the shafts and fastening the traces. The ones on horseback set off by a different way. We raced each other across the mown slopes of the vast hayfields and galloped in noisy and wine-sprung zigzags through the ricks and down a wide valley and up again through another oak spinney to the road where the carriage, trailing a long plume of dust, was trotting more sedately home, and reined in alongside.

The track followed the crest of a high ridge with the dales of Moldavia flowing away on the either hand. We were moving through illimitable sweeps of still air. Touched with pink on their undersides by the declining sun, which also combed the tall stubble with gold, one or two shoals of mackerel cloud hung motionless in the enormous sky. Whale-shaped shadows expanded along the valleys below, and the spinneys were sending long loops of shade downhill. The air was so still that the smoke from Matila Ghyka's cigar hung in a riband in the wake of our cavalcade; and how clearly the bells of the flocks, which were streaming down in haloes of golden dust to the wells and the brushwood folds a few ravines away, floated to our ears. Homing peasants waved their hats in greeting, and someone out of sight was singing one of those beautiful and rather forlorn country songs they call a *doina*. A blurred line along the sky a league away marked the itinerary of the deserting storks. Those in the carriage below were snowed under by picnic things and mushroom baskets and bunches of anemones picked in the wood. It was a moment of peace and tranquillity and we rode on in silence towards the still far-off samovar and the oil lamps and heaven knew what bad news. The silence was suddenly broken by an eager exclamation from Matila.

'Oh look!' he cried. One hand steadied the basket of mushrooms on his lap, the other pointed at the sky into which he was peering. High overhead some waterbirds, astray from the delta, perhaps, or from some nearby fen, were flying in a phalanx. (I shall have to improvise names and details here, for precise memory and ornithological knowledge both fail me. But the gist and the spirit are exact.)

'Yes,' he said, 'it's rather rare; the *Xiphorhyncus paludinensis minor*, the *glaivionette*, or Lesser Swamp Swordbill – *Wendischer Schwertvogel* in German, *glodnic* in Moldavian dialect; I believe the Wallachians call it *spadună de baltă*. Varieties are dotted about all over the world but always in very small numbers. They live in floating nests and have a very shrill ascending note in the mating season.' He whistled softly once or twice. 'Their eggs are a ravishing colour, a lovely lapis lazuli with little primrose speckles. They have been identified with the Stymphalian birds that Hercules killed, and there's a mention of them in Lucian's *Dialogues* and in Pliny the Elder, and I think in Oppian. . . . The ancient Nubians revered them as minor gods and there's *supposed* to be one on a bas-relief at Cyrene; there's certainly a flight of them in the background of a *Journey of the Magi* by Sassetta – he probably saw them in the reeds of Lake Trasimene, where they still breed; and the chiefs of two tribes on the Zambezi wear robes of their tail feathers for the new moon ceremonies. Some people,' he continued, with a slight change of key, 'find them too fishy. It's not true, as I learnt years ago near Bordeaux. On a spit, over a very slow fire – of hornbeam twigs, if possible – with frequent basting and plenty of saffron, *glaivionette à la landaise* can be delicious. . . . Alas: I've only eaten it once. . . .'

His dark eyes, a-kindle with memory, watched the birds out of sight across the dying sky, and we all burst out laughing. The cosmic approach. . . . It had been a happy day, as we had hoped, and it had to last us for a long time, for the next day's news scattered this little society for ever.

Patrick Leigh Fermor

Fourth of June Picnic

PATRICK LINDSAY

Agars Plough. Eton. Fourth of June 1946. Celebrating King George III's birthday.

The Chairman and the Director of the National Gallery entertain some of their children to a picnic luncheon. Their wives sit on the running board of the exotic V12 cylinder Lagonda Open Tourer.

In the background the soothing snick of leather on willow – the Eton eleven playing their annual cricket match against the Ramblers. Peace – and peacetime at last!

It had been a poor summer. Home-grown strawberries had not been up to scratch. Ours were flown from Israel. Cream obtained with a struggle. My first ever *pâté en croûte*.

Pâté en Croûte

Dough	*Pâté*	12 oz (350 g)
1½ lb (700 g) flour	8 oz (225 g) veal	lean ham
1 teaspoon salt	8 oz (225 g) lean pork	12 oz (350 g)
4 oz (110 g) lard	8 oz (225 g) fat pork	tongue
4 oz (110 g) butter	2 eggs	1 tin truffles
1 egg	Pepper	Aspic
½ cup cold water	2 tablespoons cognac	Parsley

Mix together the dough ingredients and wrap in waxed paper. Store overnight in the refrigerator.

Line a springform loaf tin with the dough and bake at gas mark 7 (425° F, 220° C) for 10 minutes. Then remove, and reduce the heat to gas mark 6 (400° F, 200° C). Mince together the veal, lean pork and fat pork. Add 2 eggs, Mix well, and pound to a smooth paste. Add salt and pepper. Ignite 2 tablespoons of warmed cognac and stir in. Press the forcemeat through a sieve or purée it in a blender. Cut the ham and tongue into sticks or batons about 1 inch (2.5 cm) thick and as long as possible. Cut the contents of a can of truffles into smaller sticks.

Cover the bottom of the loaf tin with a layer of forcemeat. Arrange parallel rows of truffle and ham and tongue sticks down the length of the tin. Cover these with a layer of forcemeat and proceed in this fashion until full, arranging pink and black batons to make a cross-section pattern when the pâté is sliced. Cover with a thin layer of larding pork and with the remaining dough. Decorate the crust and insert a pie funnel. Make a small hole in the centre of the covering to allow steam to escape.

Bake the pâté for about 1½ hours, brushing it once or twice with *dorure* (mix 1 tablespoon milk with beaten egg) and covering it with heavy buttered paper if it browns too quickly. Cool in the tin. Pour cool but liquid aspic through the hole in the crust to fill spaces created by shrinking during cooking. Chill the pâté well. Garnish with aspic cutouts and ribbons of finely minced parsley and aspic, stirred to fragments with a fork.

Picnic at the Glen

RODDY LLEWELLYN

Style is something sadly lacking these days, but picnics at the Glen have more than their fair share of it. One magic day, several summers ago, the two main ingredients to ensure a successful luncheon picnic were there – sun and water. Delicious home-made pâtés, pies with thick crusts and galantines made possible the coming of *La Grande Bouffe* to Loch Eddy. Gin and tonics tinkling with ice mingled with the conversation which often exploded into laughter. What seemed like an inexhaustible supply of chilled wine helped to wash down the kipper pâté and galantine of grouse, while huge bowls of salad were accompanied by a collection of stalwart cheeses which would have placated Mighty Mouse in his angriest mood. Lunch ended in a bonfire, a gentle row round Loch Eddy and a snooze on a rug or a walk. Whatever one did, one did it without a care in the world.

Kipper Pâté

7 oz (200 g) tin kipper fillets (preferably John West),
  with most of the oil drained off
1 packet aspic
Juice of half a large lemon
1 large carton cream

Put the kippers, ½ pint (275 ml) aspic, the lemon juice and cream in a liquidizer. When smooth put into an entrée dish and cool in the refrigerator for 45 minutes. Then cover with a little aspic. Decorate with parsley and eat with brown toast.

Galantine of Grouse

4 oz (110 g) calves' liver	Chopped parsley
8 oz (225 g) veal or sausage meat	Shallots
	Bay leaf
1 lb (450 g) fat pork	Garlic
4 rashers bacon	Breast of three grouse

Preheat the oven to gas mark 5 (375° F, 190° C). Put everything through the mincer except the bayleaf, bacon and grouse. Put the bayleaf at the bottom of the dish, then alternate layers of veal or sausage meat, grouse and bacon. Cook for about an hour then press down with a plate. Eat cold.

Roderic Llewellyn

'Caldo e Cremoso'

RUPERT LOEWENSTEIN

Although, like many spoilt men, I prefer the pleasures of the table in the great indoors, there can be exceptions. The pleasures of the table embrace not only what is to be eaten and drunk, but also the civilized enjoyment of good company in an attractive and comfortable setting. Increasingly I have found that wit flourishes in an atmosphere of good food and drink. Perhaps that is because I have never known (and indeed, do they still exist?) the salons where brilliant conversation is enjoyed, while the guests are only fortified by warm lemonade and, perhaps, a plate of 'fingers'.

In a happier age, in the days of good King Idris, we stayed with Italian friends in Tripoli. The day after we arrived we were taken in a bus to look at the ruins of Sabratha, some sixty or seventy miles away across the desert. Having admired the antique splendours for an hour or two in the scorching sun, our hostess asked us whether we were ready for luncheon. Thereupon we rounded a corner and saw set up in front of the huge pillars looking onto the sea a table covered with gleaming linen and, behind comfortable chairs, two footmen in neat white coats with appropriately armorial buttons.

What did we eat and drink? Cool white wine from Maser, hot cannelloni, *vitello tonnato*, some cheese with North African bread, and grapefruit sorbet. The unexpectedness in the desert of this luxury, which originally we had taken to be a mirage, and the pleasure of the company of great friends in beautiful surroundings, was such as to make it one of the most enjoyable luncheons I have ever had.

When we complimented our hostess on the delights of the day, she said, 'Always remember, for a picnic some of the food must be "caldo e cremoso".'

Rupert Loewenstein

Picnics from the Past

DOROTHY LYGON

Picnics played a definite part in our lives when we were young. They fell into two categories – nursery outings, which were ordinary nursery teas taken to the garden, the woods or the beach, or family picnics which were rarer and more elaborate, often including some of the household. I remember one of the latter sort on a steamer on the River Severn and another by the weir on the Teme. A third was on the Goodwin Sands, off the Kent coast, large areas of which are uncovered during the extreme tides of spring and autumn. The remains of a German submarine wrecked there during the 1914–18 War were still visible in the 1920s; the sand was quite firm to walk on as long as there was no water on it, otherwise it shifted round one's feet and started to engulf them in a way that was both frightening and exciting.

The food on these grown-up picnics was always the same, but they didn't happen often enough for us to get bored with it. There were bridge rolls filled with Russian salad, small mutton pies known as Buckingham Palace pies, jam puffs and coffee and chocolate éclairs. The mutton pies were particularly good. There was no need for knives, forks or spoons and I can't remember any being provided. I think we drank lemonade; the men would have had beer or whisky or cider – certainly not wine, nor do I remember ice. For a later recipe the following is one which has evolved over the last year or two; it can be used for sandwiches (made with brown bread well buttered), or put in small ramekins or cartons to eat on its own.

Allow 1½ eggs per person if the eggs are large, or 2 if small.

Hard-boil them and, after peeling, chop roughly and tip them into a roomy bowl. Add salt, pepper, a good sprinkle of Worcester sauce and enough single cream to moisten the mixture. Next add herbs, some kind of onion (either chives cut with scissors or spring onions or minced shallots), then parsley and/or whatever you have available – dill, chervil, tarragon and fennel are all good. Sometimes I have added chopped shrimps or prawns quite successfully. It can be made in advance and kept under clingfilm or foil in the refrigerator. I have not tried freezing it, but have found it a good flexible basic recipe.

Buckingham Palace Pies

Short pastry
Cooked mutton, beef, chicken   Rich gravy
  or rabbit   Butter
2 shallots, finely chopped   Stock

Preheat the oven to gas mark 7 (425° F, 220° C). Make a number of tartlet cases about the size of mince pies. Cut out two circles, one smaller than the other, for the tops of the tartlets. Cut a hole in the smaller of the circles. Bake blind until lightly browned.

Cut slices of cooked meat into small squares, rejecting any fat or sinew. Cook two finely chopped shallots in butter and mix with the meat in a pan with enough stock to cover it. It should then be cooked slowly for about an hour until the meat is extremely tender. Remove the meat, cover with a good rich brown gravy seasoned with salt, pepper and a dash of Worcester sauce, and fill the cases with this mixture. Put a little meat jelly on the top, cover with the pastry circles, one on top of the other, and fill the hole with beef jelly.

Mamie's Comfort

Fill a large thermos with hot Bovril mixed to required strength and lace generously with port and brandy. A very useful hot drink for a cold picnic.

Picnic at Hampton Court

HRH THE PRINCESS MARGARET

Nearly all picnics in Britain end up in a layby by the road because, in desperation, no one can decide where to stop. I felt that another sort of treat, slightly different and rather more comfortable, was indicated. In my opinion picnics should always be eaten at table and sitting on a chair. Accordingly my picnic, in May 1981, took the form of an outing to Hampton Court.

This mysterious palace is like nothing else – very complex in structure and design. Built first by Cardinal Wolsey, it continued in construction through many reigns. One can wander through buildings dating from about 1514 to Charles II, William and Mary (with the help of Sir Christopher Wren), and George II. George III, when faced with the choice between it and Windsor Castle, mercifully chose the latter, as Hampton Court is rather like a haphazard village.

The Queen kindly let me take some friends. The best plan, it seemed to me, was to do some sightseeing and have lunch in the middle. So I got in touch with Sir Oliver Millar, Surveyor of the Queen's Pictures, who delighted in taking us round the recently restored Mantegnas which are housed in their own Orangery. These were saved, happily, from the disastrous sale of Charles I's pictures by Cromwell, simply because Cromwell liked them.

I asked Professor Jack Plumb, Master of Christ's College, Cambridge, who had helped in writing the television series *Royal Heritage*, where we should best have our cold collation. He suggested the little Banqueting House overlooking the Thames. This seemed an excellent place for a number of reasons. It wasn't open to the public then, it was shelter in case of rain and, as far as anyone knew, there hadn't been a jolly there since the time of Frederick, Prince of Wales.

The Banqueting House used to be called the Water Gallery and was a retreat for Mary II. When she died William III pulled it down, because memories were too poignant, and built the Banqueting House on the same site. In the main room the walls and ceiling are by Verrio. The hall and ante-rooms are tiny, and being quite small it is nice and cosy. As three sides of it are surrounded by a sunken garden smelling warmly of wistaria and wallflowers, with the river flowing beneath its windows on the fourth side, it provided an ideal setting.

I took my butler to ensure that everything would be all right.

We started with smoked salmon mousse, followed by that standby of the English, various cold meats and beautiful and delicious salads. Those with room then had cheeses.

We drank a toast to Frederick, Prince of Wales and departed to inspect the famous old vine which has its own greenhouse and Nanny gardener. After that we wandered among the many visitors from abroad, round the lovely gardens and canals, viewing all the different façades of its many sides. We visited the chapel (redecorated by Wren) and the tennis court where we watched a game of royal or real tennis.

It was altogether a glorious day. The sun was shining on one of its brief appearances that summer, and everyone was happy.

Avocado Soup

3–4 avocado pears (depending on size)
1 pint (570 ml) chicken consommé
½ teaspoonful black pepper, salt and sugar mixed together
Pinch of garlic salt
1 teaspoonful Worcester sauce
A little dry sherry
Double cream

Put all the ingredients except the cream in blender. Leave in refrigerator for an hour or until very cold. Serve in consommé cups with a little dab of double cream on each serving.

Margaret

Picnic Command

GREGORY MARTIN

There are two grocers in the village. The one near the new art gallery, with its polished pine interior, has Volvos outside and espadrilles within. The cheeses on their straw platters ooze in the summer heat; the proprietor (had he been in insurance for all those years harbouring the inner Fauchon?) is a member of the golf club. But for picnic provisions we go to the other end of the village, past the recently converted Methodist chapel (now the off-licence where artist's brushes and paints mingle with bottles of wine). Then on past the coal merchant's yard which backs onto a huge field (this year a sweep of wheat), as far as the garage whose two sturdy pumps would be happiest catering for Austin Sevens. There, opposite, is the village supermarket in the old Co-op mould, where the wasps hover drowsily over the bruised plums.

No, we can't take Angel Delight on the picnic and we've still got Rich Tea biscuits over from yesterday. We need the soft, sliced white bread in its transparent wrapper; it should feel like a forgotten balloon the day after a children's party. The New Zealand butter will take hours to soften straight out of the fridge, so we'll take the marge, although you can tell the difference. Sausages – pork and beef – eggs (check that none is broken in the container), tomatoes (careful now, they cost as much as a packet of Hamlets), a bumper packet of Penguins, apples – or bananas? Watch the wasps; no plums and no, we can't eat peaches on the picnic, and no, no grapes – they'll get squashed.

All right, then, one liquorice stick – no, two.

The eggs will take as long to cook as the sausages to grill, for they will have to be hard-boiled and then thoroughly doused under a jet of cold water. It will also take longer to boil six eggs rather than, say, two, as there is that much more water in the pan. The knife can slip in the greasy wrapper round the sausages which have to be separated and then delicately pronged with a fork and not gashed by the kitchen knife. The grill not too high and pray to God no egg bursts.

Is there a surgeon in the house? Cutting up the tomatoes and the remains of the cucumber is fun.

Now for the brisk deftness of a beautician – wait, sausages not burning? – the bread slices are delicate and easily bruised, so don't squodge one up to look like the Incredible Hulk's discarded wad of chewing gum. Turn the sausages. Now spread the slices and pack the bits of tomato and cucumber symmetrically on to the pock-marked surfaces massaged with foundation cream, cover, and press with the palm of the hand (did I wash it?). Do that eight times and that should be enough for our lot. Turn off the grill; put the pan of eggs into the sink and turn on the cold tap. Not too much. Do I hear the gentle play of a fountain in the courtyard of a Florentine palazzo? Where is everyone? Let's get this show on the road, Kraemer.

The sausages are not burnt. Place them in silver foil – don't think of that picnic in David Storey's novel – now wrap them up. This is more our sporting life. Call for the fine art packers. Or am I a fur-coated jeweller carefully arranging Fabergé eggs and layers of ruby and emerald bracelets, wrapped in tissue paper, in my Gucci travelling case? The plastic lid does fit if you slot it on taking each side individually, although you will need a little extra pressure to align the last two edges. The pale green box looks clinically neat; and the bunch of bananas placed on it would add an artistic touch. Plastic cups? No time to clear up the mess.

Our friends have arrived. This is the Strategic Picnic Command. Stores are loaded – don't forget the tennis ball – as the corps commanders confer and fix a rendezvous: the public car park by the links. And the tanks roll out across the desert. I'll shut the sun roof unless you all sit down; it's dangerous to stand. Hold on to Rosey, for goodness' sake.

From afar, the car park is a dazzle of reflected sunlight. We queue to pay the attendant in his white coat. Despatch a detail to buy Coca-Cola and salted, not onion-flavoured, crisps. No, we can't have ice creams until after the picnic. We stumble over the dunes – *Ice Cold in Alex*; the youngest recruit, pants still dry, is carried shoulder-high as we approach our path of El Alamein, hot and weary, passing corpses lying in the sun near enemy dugouts. Only one pretty girl in sight. But the sea is flat and azure bright, and there is not a cloud in the sky. Let's all swim and then have our picnic.

Gregory Martin

A Boating Picnic in Overy Staithe

MARIT MAUFE

My husband has a dingy and so have I. We love them dearly but, each being 12 feet long, having tiny cockpits and booms that threaten to hit you on the head when you go about, they are not very good boats in which to sit and eat a picnic. So we have to climb into other people's boats when we want to eat more than an apple.

Cockles are a great favourite with us, except when they are drowned in vinegar. Here is a cockle dish which I first enjoyed in a fado house in Lisbon; I have since put it together from taste and memory. We feel puddings are not very boaty things, and prefer cakes, which are much easier to deal with.

Cockles and Pork

1 pint (570 ml) cockles per person
2–3 pieces lean pork per person
1 lb (450 g) onions, peeled and sliced
1½ lb (700 g) tomatoes (if tinned pour off liquid)
½ pint (275 ml) oil

Rinse the cockles free from sand. Spread in a large basin or sink, barely cover with salty water, and leave for 2–3 hours. Finally rinse thoroughly under running water. Open the cockles in very little boiling water, not too many at a time. When finished, strain the cooking liquid through a fine sieve and set aside. Combine onions, tomatoes and oil in a saucepan, bring to the boil and leave to simmer gently for a least 30 minutes. Hammer the lean pork very thin. Use no salt. Fry quickly in a little oil, and put the pieces aside. Use some of the cockle liquid to deglaze the frying pan, and add this to the tomato mixture with the cockles and the pork pieces. Mix everything carefully together, adding more cockle liquid if you wish. The finished dish should have a fair amount of 'soup'. Taste for seasoning.

Apple Cake

2 eggs
7 oz (200 g) sugar
8 oz (225 g) butter
8 oz (225 g) self-raising flour
2 teaspoons baking powder
1½ lb (700 g) apples, peeled and cut in wedges

Preheat the oven to gas mark 5 (375° F, 190° C). Beat eggs and add the sugar. Add the softened butter, flour and baking powder. Grease a fireproof dish. Put in the apples and cover with the cake mixture. Bake for about ¾–1 hour until golden brown and serve in the tin. If you eat this cake at home you might like to serve it with a vanilla cream.

Vanilla Cream

1 egg
1 tablespoon sugar
1 tablespoon cornflour
½ pint (275 ml) creamy milk
Vanilla essence
Whipped cream (optional)

Mix all the ingredients well together except the vanilla essence and the cream. Put into a small heavy saucepan, and heat gently, stirring constantly, until it thickens. *Do not boil.* If you find this operation difficult, use a double boiler. Remove from the heat, add vanilla to taste, and whip occasionally until cool. To make a lighter mixture fold in some whipped cream.

Garry's Punch

1 pint (570 ml) hot China tea   1 gill (145 ml) green Chartreuse
½ pint (285 ml) brandy   1 gill (145 ml) calves' foot jelly
½ pint (285 ml) rum   Juice of two limes
1 gill (145 ml) Grand Marnier   Sugar to taste

Mix all ingredients together and warm. Do *not* heat above 174° F, 79° C, otherwise the alcohol will evaporate.

Marit Maufe.

Marchmont Picnic

CECILIA McEWEN

The picnic for me conjures up idyllic scenes under trees, dappled shade, a rippling stream, with girls in muslin and men in panama hats. Baskets of food, French bread and white wine. This illusion has been spitefully dashed by the Scottish Border climate, where many a memorable picnic has been endured, huddled under the walls of Hermitage Castle, the beauty of which has been shrouded in mist, rain mingling with a fried egg sarnie, and a snell wind anaesthetizing the fingers.

Picnics now usually take place on the lawn, where a quick dash for cover can be organized at a moment's notice. A table helps to stop any spillages brought on by uneven surfaces or a surfeit of Bloody Marys. Paper everything (no regrets) – cloth, plates, cups and napkins – and burn the lot at the end. A piece of lamb barbecuing, smelling of rosemary, garlic and cognac. Crisp lettuce, cut very thick, to dip in either dressing or fresh mayonnaise; a personal adaptation of a Spanish omelette which can be cooked and remain in a quiche dish and be eaten with fingers. A terrine to slap on some French bread while waiting for the lamb to cook. Some radishes, some cream cheese with freshly chopped herbs, apples, butter, salt and a large pepper grinder.

Finally, vital to cooks and guests alike, a great deal of drink. Cold white wine, beer, cider and apple juice.

One eccentricity carried on from childhood at Marchmont is the marmalade sandwich – it has to be at every picnic. This may sound unappetizing, but can be interesting if made with brown bread, butter and chunky marmalade. There has to be a plentiful supply as addicts will eat them throughout the picnic, beginning as a first course and finishing up what is left as a sort of pudding.

Papillon of Lamb for Barbecue (Mr McEwen's Special)

A small leg of lamb, boned by the butcher so that when opened flat it resembles the shape of a butterfly. Marinate in brandy, olive oil, rosemary, crushed garlic and pepper. Seal on each side quickly on the barbecue. It should be pink in the centre when cooked. Cut on a bread board in slices like an entrecôte.

Terrine of Game or Veal

6–8 rashers streaky bacon	Parsley, marjoram, thyme
8 oz (225 g) pig's liver	8 oz (225 g) pie veal or
1 small onion	breasts of pheasant
1 clove garlic	8 oz (225 g) pork fat
8 oz (225 g) sausage meat	Salt and pepper

Preheat the oven to gas mark 4 (350° F, 180° C). Line a baking dish with bacon rashers. Mince the pork, liver, onion and garlic, add the sausage meat and herbs and mix well. Spread half the liver mixture over the bacon in the dish. Arrange strips of veal or pheasant on top. Cover with the remaining liver mixture. Cover the pan with foil. Place in a larger dish containing water and cook for one hour.

Turn out while still warm and drain excess fat.

Cecilia McEwen.

An Irish Picnic

THE McGILLYCUDDY OF THE REEKS

Kerry picnics by their very nature are liable to be held in the rain, courtesy of the Atlantic Ocean and the high mountains. Undeterred, however, and always saying 'Oh, it will get better' (which it sometimes does), we often troop off bravely armed with suitable refreshments both liquid and solid.

Though varying from picnic to picnic, we would take such things as Killorglin oak-smoked salmon and delicious soda bread, fresh farm eggs hard-boiled, Kerry lamb and/or beef in puff pastry, fresh salad and avocados. Should we go to the lake, a barbecue of sausages, steaks or lamb chops can be cooked over a turf fire with a little help from wood to stop the food tasting entirely of turf smoke. To drink we inevitably take a large supply of Guinness, and then have coffee laced liberally with Irish whiskey.

I love chutney and will put it with almost anything (but not smoked salmon of course), and here is the recipe.

Chutney

4 lb (1.8 kg) tomatoes
3 lb (1.35 kg) apples
8 oz (225 g) shallots
1 lb (450 g) sultanas
1 lb (450 g) brown
  sugar

3 pints (1 litre 700 ml)
  malt vinegar
1 oz (25 g) salt
½ oz (10 g) bruised
  ginger
Chillies

Chop the tomatoes, the peeled apples and shallots and mix them in a large pan with 2 pints (1 litre 140 ml) of the vinegar, chopped bruised ginger, chillies, salt and sultanas. Cook till the fruit is soft, then add the remaining vinegar and the sugar. Cook for approximately 3–4 hours until the consistency is smooth, then bottle in clean, dry jars.

J. Tilly cuddy.

The Stalkers' Picnic Lunch

JOHN NOBLE

The first important requirement is a folding lunch tin. If you go to the hill with your rations in a paper bag or wrapped in greaseproof paper you will find that, when the tactiturn stalker who has been conducting operations announces, often in a dramatic whisper, 'We'll tek our piece the noo', a soggy bundle will emerge from the ghillie's bag, a curious lumpen mass in which the boiled egg, the sardine and jam sandwiches and chocolate biscuit have been blended together in an unappetizing *macedoine*. Quarter-mile crawls up rocky burns and through peat bogs demand suitable protection for your picnic lunch. A *folding* tin (large pocket size) is thus essential. It takes up less space in a bag when collapsed and does not crush easily if given rough treatment.

Now we can consider the correct choice of food and drink appropriate to the occasion. It should be realized that lunch may well be a rushed moment. Spirits may be low, perhaps after a miss; the body tired, cold and both hungry and thirsty.

The experienced hill man avoids drinking from every burn because a thirst often increases once you start to lap water. So, even if there are many burns around, you should avoid foods likely to make you thirsty. Smoked salmon, Marmite, kipper pâté, *petit sâle*, and even certain salty cures of hams should be avoided. Sandwiches tend to be stodgy and often dry. Dank sliced bread filled with salad mixture or beige, tinned luncheon meat, or bread acting as a sort of blotting paper drying out the jam, can bring tears to the eyes of the gourmet 'rifle' who has just missed a 'Royal' and faces a testy and demanding host on his return.

Aim at something to look forward to, something tempting and restoring. Keep it simple and compact – complicated charcuterie and fragile patisserie are out of place. An ideal lunch – the theme can of course be varied – which packs easily into the folding tin might comprise several slices of thickly carved underdone beef or saddle of lamb or fillet of venison. These should not be clamped between pieces of steam-baked bread, but should be wrapped in greaseproof paper on their own. A good slice of well-buttered, home-baked brown bread, made from stone-ground flour, should be packed alongside. Two or three Scotch tomatoes from the cold house are most refreshing and thirst-quenching. Fill the tin finally with as large a piece of *Gâteau Négresse*, a moist rich chocolate cake, as it will accommodate. A crisp apple can be carried in the pocket, likewise a bar of dark chocolate.

A small flask of good, malty, blended whisky, not less than eight years old, is recommended. A nip taken as an aperitif, a nip as a digestif, and a couple of nips reserved for the moment of ultimate triumph or disappointment, are all that is required. Avoid too large a flask. It will unsteady your aim or make you over-confident and boastful.

With these few simple rules of gastronomy your happiness and your success on the hill are likely to be enhanced. That important moment, some time between twelve o'clock and two, when the 'pieces' are brought out, will be one of keen anticipation, even if, by ill luck or lack of skill, you seem destined for a stalk *manqué*, and the cold is beginning to numb.

Gâteau Négresse
(Rich Chocolate Cake)

6 oz (175 g) plain chocolate
6 oz (175 g) caster sugar
3 oz (75 g) ground almonds
5 eggs

2 oz (50 g) self-raising flour
White fondant or glâcé icing flavoured with rum

Preheat the oven to gas mark 3 (325° F, 160° C). Break up the chocolate and melt it over a gentle heat. Cream the butter, add the sugar and beat until soft and white. Separate the eggs. Beat in the chocolate with the almonds and egg yolks. Whip the whites stiffly and fold in the flour. Bake for 45–50 minutes.

When cold, ice with a white fondant or glâcé icing flavoured with rum.

John Noble

Sahara Picnics

JOHN JULIUS NORWICH

I love picnics; indeed, I once had 147 of them running. That was in 1966, when I spent seven weeks crossing and re-crossing the Sahara. As far as I remember I enjoyed them all – all, at least, except two, because they had to be eaten during a sandstorm, and the sand always managed to get into one's mouth before anything else did.

There were seven of us, in the capable hands of a first-class *Saharien* guide, Jean Sudriez, who knew better than anyone the secrets of successful desert catering. These include one great fundamental truth: that the food provided for expeditions like ours should be not only nourishing but, within the limits imposed by the circumstances, good. The Sahara demands austerities enough, and there is no point in adding to them unnecessarily. He had accordingly scoured the *épiceries* of Algiers, and loaded one of our three Land Rovers to overflowing with as wide a variety of tinned delicacies as they were able to produce – to be supplemented of course by bread, dates and occasional supplies of other fruit and vegetables from the oases along our way.

The breakfast menu was determined by the need to get the blood circulating again after the almost indescribable cold of the desert night – for the air has no moisture in it to retain the heat, and the thermometer plummets after sunset. We would wake up frozen to the marrow, to be revived (as soon as we had got the fire going) by bowls of steaming porridge, washed down by Nescafé or, more often, a delicious Ovaltine-like drink called Banania – which I vaguely remembered having seen advertised, but had never drunk before and have never tasted since. Bread was a rarity; but we had *biscottes*, Ryvita, tinned butter and industrial quantities of jam.

That would be at about six in the morning; lunch, however, was a more moveable feast, for by nine the sun was literally searing off every inch of skin left unprotected and we would simply stop wherever some unusual feature of the landscape offered the chance of a bit of shade. At high noon, such blessings are rare. The sun blazes down from immediately above one's head, and, in the absence of any trees outside an oasis, the best that can usually be hoped for is some little outcrop of rock with a few overhangs beneath which to huddle. Sometimes we would stretch an awning between two Land Rovers; but the Sahara is a windy place and the operation was seldom as easy as it sounds. Once settled, we would dig into the usual picnic fare – pilchards and pâté, liverwurst and cheese; but the real pleasure came afterwards, with the cool and sloshy – the tinned asparagus, the peperoni and fruit salad that slip down parched throats like a benediction, caressing and refreshing as they go. No wine at lunchtime; in such heat it would have destroyed us, and we didn't even want it. But the water was wonderful because, thanks to our *guerbas*, it was always cold.

The *guerba* is a wonderful thing. A swollen, still furry and all too recognizable carcase of a goat may not be the most attractive of containers for one's drinking water, but its porousness permits just the right degree of evaporation to keep the contents cool, and its position on the outside of the car gives it the full benefit of the breeze. It hangs upside down, by what used to be the legs; a small plug, inevitably if somewhat indelicately placed at one end, serves as a tap. Cold running water in the Sahara noonday, whatever its taste, colour or provenance, is a commodity not to be despised. We each drank well over a gallon a day.

By nightfall it would be cold again, and there would be a new edge to the wind. The fire would be lit – we never missed the occasional opportunity to stock up with firewood or dried bracken, any more than we did with water – and a few more of our precious tins would be emptied into the pot: spaghetti perhaps, or lentils, or chilli con carne as the *pièce de résistance*, with the usual concomitants of sausage, tuna fish and cheese, rounded off with a few succulent spoonfuls of condensed milk flavoured with caramel or Grand Marnier and washed down with vin rosé. Those dinners were for me one of the high spots of the day. We would go on sitting round the fire for as long as it lasted, then put on every available sweater, zip ourselves into first our woollen tracksuits and then our sleeping bags, and sleep under the stars till it was time for breakfast again.

Such was the basic régime on which we covered some eight hundred miles of desert; and even when we found ourselves in the Tibesti Mountains and had to abandon our Land Rovers for camels it did not change appreciably; the only difference was that camel milk suddenly became available as an optional extra. For two or three days after stopping in an oasis we might supplement it with fresh bread, lettuce and tomatoes, and once we were able to buy a whole *guerba* stuffed full of date paste – which, scooped out with the fingers and carried straight to the mouth, was one of the memorable gastronomic pleasures of my life. But these were bonuses. Tins were the staple, and it is hard to see how we could possibly have improved on them. There was only one serious misfortune that we were called upon to suffer: the vin rosé ran out after five and a half weeks. But by then, hardened *Sahariens* that we were, we had learned to take disaster in our stride.

Washing up was never a problem. Though water was naturally far too precious to waste on such a purpose, the desert did every bit as well. One dug the plate or fork or mug into the sand, scoured it round for a moment, and the job was done as well as in any kitchen sink. The sand also solved the problem of what to do with the rubbish. We buried it carefully about a foot deep, then carefully smoothed over the place until there was no sign left of where it had been. This sort of habit is every bit as important in the deep Sahara as anywhere else – perhaps even more so, since in that dryness nothing ever decays. Once outside the oases, the desert is the cleanest place in the world; and it is also, to me at least, one of the most beautiful. It has a sparkling purity about it unlike anywhere else I have been; one longs for it to remain like that for ever.

A Salmon-Fishing Picnic in Wales

MOLLIE PHILIPPS

True devotees of salmon fishing look upon any interruption of their sport as unthinkable. A quick sandwich, perhaps, while changing a fly or minnow, an apple while working out a strategy for attacking the next pool, but nothing more. One of the keenest I know used to ask the ghillie to wade out to where he stood, like Jeremy Fisher waist-deep in mid-stream, and feed him with bars of chocolate while he continued to cast. He loved sweet things, and thus managed to satisfy two passions at once – a happy man.

Slightly less dedicated anglers slip off surreptitiously at midday to the local pub, seductively sited on a nearby bank and providing an excellent ploughman's lunch and draught cider. On wet days and windy days this break can be prolonged until closing time.

However, perhaps the best solution, when the weather is fine, is a picnic on the river bank. In the old days these used to be mounted in grand style; silver flasks for pre-lunch whiskies, white tablecloths and a butler to carry out the house specialities of mutton patties and potted salmon. Alas! The recipes died with Mrs Bones, the cook; the butler departed, and now things are much simpler.

During a recent unexpectedly hot and sunny Easter weekend we decided to try and re-create something of this atmosphere. The chosen spot was a particularly beautiful stretch of the Upper Wye, which is wide but has rapids that make it more like an American or Canadian river than a mere tame British one. A stream, the Bach Howey, rushes into it at this point and below their junction is a particularly good salmon pool.

The fishermen had been flogging away here unsuccessfully all morning and seemed rather pleased when the large group arrived. This was just as well, for among the hampers, Indian tablecloths and fur rugs was a wind-up gramophone with four records including 'The way you look tonight' and 'Love walked in', which been spotted in a junk shop that morning and triumphantly carried away. The result was a picnic-*dansant*, noisy enough to scare away the laziest or deafest fish.

We ate smoked salmon sandwiches (poor taste from the salmon's point of view, but there is an excellent smokery in Hereford), trout from the Bach Howey smoked on the Abu Smoker, a re-creation, based on family memories, of the mutton patties and potted salmon of Mrs Bones, coleslaw salad, a truckle Cheddar and fruit. White wine was cooled in the icy water of the stream.

Curried Mutton Patties

These are small pies and can either be taken to the picnic hot, wrapped in a napkin, or eaten cold. They can be made with flaky pastry or with hot water crust as for pork pies.

Pastry

8 oz (225 g) flour	Cold water
6 oz (175 g) margarine	1 egg
Pinch of salt	

Filling

1 lb (450 g) lean mutton	Salt, pepper
preferably from the leg	Peppercorns
Bouquet garni	2 tablespoons diced carrots
2 onions stuck with	1 tablespoon diced potato
2 cloves	2 teaspoons curry powder

Make a pastry with the above pastry ingredients. Preheat the oven to gas mark 7 (425° F, 220° C).

Put the mutton in a stew pan with the bouquet garni, onions stuck with cloves, salt and peppercorns. Barely cover with cold water, bring to the boil, skim and simmer until just tender. Allow to cool in the stock. Put the diced carrot and onion into a pan. Strain enough stock from the lamb to cover, simmer for 5 minutes, then add the diced potato. Continue simmering until the vegetables are just cooked. Drain, keeping the stock, and turn into a bowl. Dice the mutton and add to the vegetables with a little stock to moisten, and curry powder and seasoning to taste. Divide the pastry in half, roll out one half and line a greased patty tin. Stamp out into rounds and cover the pies, first wetting the edges of the pastry. Press round the edges, decorate and brush with beaten egg. Bake for 20–30 minutes. Remove the patties from the tins and cool slightly before packing.

Potted Salmon

Take equal proportions of salmon and clarified butter. For every 8 oz (225 g) of salmon take 6 oz (175 g) of butter and reduce to a paste in the blender. Season, pack tightly down into a pot or pots, smooth over the top, cover, and leave in the refrigerator until very firm. Melt 3 oz (75 g) clarified butter and pour it when tepid over the salmon paste so that it sets in a sealing layer about ⅛ inch (3 mm) thick. When completely cold, cover the pots. The potted salmon should be served chilled with fresh bread or made into sandwiches.

Clarified Butter

Put a slab of butter into a large frying pan or sauté pan. Let it melt over a very gentle heat. It must not brown, but should be allowed to bubble for a few seconds. Remove from the heat and leave to settle. Wring out a piece of butter muslin (or surgical gauze) in warm water, double it and lay in a sieve standing over the bowl or jar in which the butter is to be stored. Filter the butter while still warm, and keep the jar covered in the refrigerator.

Iced Tea

½ pint (275 ml) hot, strong tea of superior blend	Ice cubes
	2–3 lemon slices
Caster sugar to taste	Mint

Pour hot tea into jug and add sugar to taste. Stir until all sugar has dissolved. Add some ice cubes, the lemon slices and mint. Leave until tea is cold (add more tea if needed). Pour into chilled thermos. Pack more ice in an extra thermos.

Mollie Phillips

A Red Indian Picnic

DAVID PLANTE

In Tulsa, Oklahoma, there are many Red Indians. They tell you, 'I'm an eighth Indian', or '. . . a sixteenth Indian', or '. . . a thirty-fourth Indian'. They belong mostly to the Osage and Cherokee tribes. As I am an eighth Blackfoot, I thought it natural that I should go to an Indian picnic.

A Cherokee friend took me along. He did not seem to mind much that I am Blackfoot. I can't read Cherokee, so he had to translate a sign nailed to a tree: 'NO LITTERING, NO ROWDINESS, NO DRINKING'. I thought I'd better be careful among these Cherokees.

We went through the woods into a clearing.

My friend Rennard (Fox) introduced me to elderly men wearing stetson hats with eagle feathers, standing about a carefully heaped pile of white wood ash on top of which logs were burning. Rennard whispered to me, lest I ask and reveal that I was from another tribe, that this was the sacred fire. One of the old men was standing with his back to the fire, smoking a long-stemmed pipe; he puffed to make a lot of smoke, which rose up, mingling with the smoke of the fire. Rennard said to me, leaning his head close to mine, 'He is sending up smoke messages that he is a follower of the way.' This of course I understood, and I nodded. Then an old woman in a house dress puffed on the pipe, and the smoke rose.

There was a strange stillness.

Around the sacred fire were seven clan houses, open huts made of wooden pillars and wood shingle roofs, in which were benches, and the Indians of the different Cherokee clans sat in their clan houses; some houses were almost empty, some crowded. The Indians didn't move, or talk, but sat still.

Beyond the clearing in the woods was another clearing, where women in house dresses and aprons were washing huge black kettles; some of the kettles were over fires, and in the kettles pork fat and pork meat were boiling together. Rennard introduced me to the older women, not the younger; he asked them how many hogs had been slaughtered, and they said four. Dark women were stirring the kettles with long sticks.

We waited around, Rennard and I. The sunlight beamed down through the surrounding woods onto parked cars and trucks; in the clearing, there was silence and little motion. Soon, I didn't mind how long we stood around, and I lost the sense of waiting for anything. I looked out into the woods.

Then the reading of the wampum belts began.

The food was placed on a long trestle table covered with a red and white checked cloth. The men were on one side, the women on the other. The table was laden with paper plates of the pork pieces, and pots of boiled chicken and dumplings; there were devilled eggs, pickled beets, baked beans, boiled greens, corn bread, pies and large flat cakes. For drink, there was a big enamel pot of Kool Aid (orange) with a ladle, and paper cups. I asked Rennard why there was no ya-kha-pins (boiled water-lily root), and he said, 'Shush, that's Osage.' An old man said a prayer in Cherokee at the top of the table, and we each picked up a paper plate.

In the evening the Indians, men, women and children, danced about the fire. Some of the women, in flowered house dresses and aprons, wore turtle shell shakers about their lower legs; pebbles in the shells rattled as they danced. The only other sound was the singing, alternating from high cries to low grunts. The Indians who didn't dance sat on folding chairs.

Then we went home.

Devilled Eggs

As many hard-boiled eggs as required, sliced in two lengthways, laid upside-down on a serving dish and covered in the following sauce.

3–4 tablespoons gooseberry jelly
1 teaspoon lemon or orange juice
Grated rind of an orange
4–5 tablespoons good plum or tomato chutney
Pepper, salt, paprika
Chopped herbs (optional)
Cream (optional)

Mix together and beat gently. Chopped herbs and a little cream may be added if desired. Increase quantitites if necessary.

David Plante

The Kingdom of Picnics

GAIA SERVADIO

My idea of picnicking has sprung from eccentric, distant roots. When my sister and I were very small and when spring had settled on the Euganean hills, my father would assemble a few cooking pans and put them and myself on his bicycle. My sister had her own bicycle, something I didn't envy because it terrified me. The food for the picnic – and that was the excitement – was to be found and cooked *in situ*. While one of us assembled dry branches, the other would charm the friars of the Abbey of Chiaravalle, a dream of a Romanesque building, into selling us some of their freshly baked bread. The farmers would let us have a few eggs, still warm; in the fields we would gather *rucola*, that bitter, pungent leaf, and wild mint. And then we would cook.

Now that I have moved to the kingdom of picnics (Britain), my approach remains basically the same: to enjoy a picnic properly one should find the food for it, and cook it, on the spot. Not that I light a fire when I go to Glyndebourne, but I don't see the point of taking a lot of pre-cooked food, a lot of plates and a lot of people transferring it in order to eat.

My recipe for a Scottish picnic – my home is in Scotland, and most of my picnicking is done there – is as follows. A fair number of children and grown-ups, raw potatoes, salt, plenty of butter, bread and a frying pan. Very fresh trout (still alive if possible) in a plastic bag. Cheeses, thyme, pepper, knives, forks, matches and glasses. Despite the occasional tempest, downpour, gale, etc., the burns and the beauty of Scotland make it a superb picnicking land.

So now we select the ideal spot (of course, someone will discover that the next curve of the burn was better): the children gather stones and dry branches; the fire is lighted at once, while volunteers look for chanterelles and ceps (*Boletus edulis*) and others clean the trout in the burn.

Stuff the trout with thyme, salt them and cook them directly on the burning wood (turning them after five minutes). The eggs should be fried in the frying pan with the chanterelles or ceps; the bread toasted on the hot stones with the cheese on top. Nothing tastes better than food cooked on wood.

Drink: water, Scottish water, absolute delight!

At the end of this picnic everybody will be dirty and exhausted. Weather permitting, a dip in the burn is recommended.

Dartmoor Picnic

FREYA STARK

The best picnics I have known were taken during solitary rides about Dartmoor, on the back of one or other of two home-bred, intelligent animals who would stand still in the heather while I got on or off. When we felt hungry we would find a flat granite stone and I would sit and undo the sandwiches that Cook had prepared, while the black or the bay nuzzled over my shoulder for the lump of sugar that was coming. The moor spread everywhere around, dipping to its rivers, and a quiet happiness blossomed, not only across its brown and healthy spaces, but also from a familiar and beloved atmosphere of countless generations who had felt the same happiness that I was feeling now.

Freya Stark

Preparations for a Shooting Picnic at Holkham

ANNE TENNANT

On Thursday, 21 June 1979, Mrs Taylor returned to Holkham on a visit. She had been kitchen maid there from 1918 to 1920 and Mr Jolly, administrator at Holkham, had asked her to revisit the 'haunts of her youth'. Mr Jolly took some notes of her visit which he kindly passed on to me. She was born Gladys Barlow in 1900 and came to Holkham in 1918. During her stay she was never allowed in the state rooms, although on one occasion, when the family was away, a housemaid smuggled her along the ground-floor passages to peep into the Marble Hall for a few seconds. This was considered a very daring act which would have been punished if seen by any of the senior staff. Seven full-time footmen worked in the house and, when in their best livery, the powdered footmen wore black suits, yellow and black check waistcoats and white gloves. On occasions additional footmen were sent over on loan from Lord Lothian of Blickling Hall. Other staff included four kitchen maids, two kitchen porters, nine housemaids, two still-room maids and five laundry maids.

A whole carcass of lamb, calf or deer would be cooked for the household, the best cuts for the dining room or shooting picnic, next for the nursery, then senior and junior staff. One man would spend his day preparing vegetables, including 1 cwt of potatoes a day.

In the old kitchen Mrs Taylor pointed out three steamers in the recess to the right of the spit and said they were not used every day for cooking, but only for shooting lunches. The steam would be generated in the boiler below (now an incinerator) and the steamer would be used to cook fish and meat, with the four small containers for vegetables.

Shortly before midday the game cart would arrive at the porter's door and footmen would then disconnect the unions of the steamers, which were then carried to the game cart and transported to wherever lunch was being taken. Church Paddock and Scarborough Clump were favourite places.

The rules of the kitchen were such that no unauthorized person was allowed in, and for this reason the serving hatches on either side of the kitchen door were regularly in use – one for hot food and the other for cold. The main door was not used.

Another interesting memory features the boiled egg for the children's breakfast. At about 8 a.m. each morning two footmen would arrive in the kitchen with a trolley. On the trolley was a large copper container into which boiling water would be poured. An inner liner was then placed inside and this in turn would receive a number of fresh eggs. More boiling water was poured in until the eggs were completely covered. The whole was then covered with a lid and the trolley pushed from the kitchen to the nursery in the Chapel wing. The timing was such that on arrival the eggs were freshly boiled and ready for the children's breakfast.

I had great difficulty in choosing two recipes from my grandmother's own recipe book. There were so many good ones. Finally I decided on Holkham Pudding which I have never had anywhere else and a delicious venison dish which travels well and has been much appreciated when I have produced it on picnics in Scotland.

Holkham Pudding

6 oz (175 g) sifted self-raising flour
8 oz (225 g) shredded suet
2 eggs
6 oz (175 g) sultanas
5 oz (150 g) soft brown sugar
1 small cup of milk
A little caster sugar

Mix all the ingredients and beat on the lowest setting of the electric whisk for 2 minutes. Leave for 1 hour. Place in a buttered pudding basin and steam for 2 hours, then turn out on an ovenproof serving dish and sprinkle with caster sugar. Bake in a hot oven for thirty minutes. Serve with hot melted butter and chilled. This pudding tastes good cut into slices and fried in hot butter or eaten cold like a cake.

Venison Chops with Chestnut Purée

6 venison chops   ½ teaspoon pepper
1 teaspoon salt   1 tablespoon butter

Pureé
1 lb (450 g) chestnuts
½ pint (275 ml) stock
Milk to blend until right consistency is reached
1 oz (25 g) butter

Sauce
3 tablespoons redcurrant jelly
Juice of 4 oranges

Neatly trim and flatten the chops, season all over with salt and pepper. Thoroughly heat butter in a pan and add the chops. Cook for 6 minutes on each side.

Split the chestnut skins at the pointed ends and put the chestnuts into a saucepan. Cover them with water and bring to the boil. Take them out of the water and skin them. Put them back in the pan with just enough stock to cover and simmer for an hour. Pureé them by mashing with hot milk and butter. Place the purée in the middle of a dish and arrange the chops round them.

Remove fat from the first pan, add redcurrant jelly and mix thoroughly until melted. Pour in orange juice, mix well, and boil for 2 minutes. Pour the sauce over the chops.

When the dish is taken on a picnic, the chestnut purée and sauce should be carried in separate containers.

Mustique

COLIN TENNANT

A picnic is different. In a cupboard, on a hillside, up a gum tree, down among the dead men – anything out of the daily grind. Herein lies our first problem. In Mustique we have a picnic every day. Second problem, always the same people; and third, always the same food. That's not to say we don't enjoy ourselves. It's like laughing at an old joke. It gets better every time. So here goes, everyone, wait for it!

We meet at the beach.

Eenie, meenie   Lagoon or Macaroni (that's the name of the beach, not the main course). Macaroni has waves, and no sandflies. For those that can't handle the ocean, Lagoon has sandflies and no waves. For those that can't handle the sandflies, there's 'off'!

Miney, mo   Cold cuts, or chicken. The Great General Store in Mustique rarely sells a whole chicken. More usually on offer are what are termed 'chicken parts'. These are fairer than a regular chicken, because each frozen box contains a number of similar parts, i.e. all legs or all wings. There is no question of having to carve or ask guests, 'Which part would you like?' and being left oneself with a bit of brown. NB Avoid at all costs 'chicken backs'.

Catch   A coloured person (Ahem). Plenty of choice here. However, remember to tell your guests if the picnic is for somebody's birthday, or alternatively in fancy dress.

OUT   Spells out. So, as it's too hot to stay indoors, out we must go. See you.

A glance in the fridge will tell you all you need to know about cold cuts. The chicken parts are more complicated as they need defrosting and should be grilled or devilled.

Mustique Mule

1 fresh coconut (or waternut) per person
Vodka
Lime syrup

Cut off the top of the nut with a cutlass. Pour out some of the milk, pour in vodka, lime syrup and ice cubes. Drink through a straw.
   Caution: coconut milk will stain your clothes, irremediably.

Seaweed Supper

For an evening picnic on the beach, wrap whatever fresh fish is available in layers of wet seaweed and grill gently over a fire. When cooked remove the seaweed and sprinkle with fresh lime juice.

Anne's Ginger Whisky Creams or Pudding

1 tablespoon whisky
2 tablespoons syrup from stem ginger
2 tablespoons caster sugar
½ teaspoon powdered ginger
½ pint (275 ml) double cream
2 egg whites
3 pieces of stem ginger to decorate

Place the whisky, ginger syrup, powdered ginger, caster sugar and cream in a bowl and whisk with an egg beater until thick. In another bowl whisk the egg whites until stiff. Fold the egg whites into the ginger mixture, spoon into individual dishes and chill. Decorate with small pieces of chopped stem ginger. Cover with foil and pack into an insulated bag ready for the picnic.

Tuscan Picnic

VANESSA THOMAS

We hardly ever picnic in Tuscany – there is always a delectable and well-placed trattoria near the end of any expedition. Conversely, every meal is a picnic since, like all English, we eat outside whenever remotely possible. But as our picnic table is three yards from the kitchen stove, we can cheat in the matter of picnic clutter, what to pack the stuff in, what kind of plates, glasses, etc. to take, and whether or not to have something hot from the stove. We eat under a huge fig tree, the leaves very useful as fruit plates and napkins, whatever Adam and Eve did with them.

Everything must be thick and chunky except the drink. I would start with a *fettunta*, a garlicky toast, eaten hot. This, with some icy white wine, is meant to keep the picnickers at bay while things are got ready.

The thing that everybody likes and which takes a bit of time is, of course, the pizza. However you can make lots of tomato sauce in advance, so the pizza dough is the only work. In my family, every-body seems to prefer pizza relatively plain – just the sauce, some sliced tomatoes and a bit of mozzarella. It can travel in a car in its tin, not yet cut up, straight from the oven – and is equally nice, as everyone knows, hot, tepid or cold. Tuscan bean salad is a rather stodgy accompaniment but an alternative for the few non-pizza eaters. You can transport it easily in a large plastic dish with a lid, already in its dressing.

The only other essentials are Tuscan bread, Tuscan salami and pecorino cheese, and a good knife. They must all be cut as and when wanted, not in advance – the unevenness of the cutting is half the charm. The first must be white, as the *pane integrale* is not nearly so satisfactory and, I suspect, not so *integrale* as all that. The second must be that large irregular-patterned Tuscan salami full of lumps of white fat on a porphyry ground – as distinct from the smooth, flecked Milanese salami as the Cosmati marble floors of eleventh-century Italian churches are from plastic imitations in modern bathrooms. If it is a slim sausage and not a nice fat one, you can cut the slices diagonally to make them bigger, since size is important too and you don't want lots of little bits that fall off the bread. As to the third, there are many more delicious Italian cheeses but, since I have never found pecorino to travel well to England, it is only in Tuscany that one can appreciate this sheep's cheese to the full; it should not be *too* young and spongy. It should be cut like a cake, but not too generously because a little goes a long way. A large peach each should round off the picnic.

For those who don't like wine, I would make lemonade – very economical if you use some citric acid. If transporting, take a bottle of it and also a huge thermos of water and ice, but don't mix it in advance – it is nicer to get variations in the strength as you down your fifth or sixth glass after a long walk. Finally, I always take coffee – those who don't like it won't mind, those who are expecting it can't get their digestive juices to work without it. It must be made, very strong, from double roast, dark beans, preferably Brazilian.

Pizza Dough

1 lb (450 g) plain flour
1 tablespoon fresh yeast
½ pint (275 ml) hand-hot water
Margarine for greasing
Tomato sauce (see below)

Put the flour into a bowl and add the fresh yeast dissolved in the water (in Italy this is normally done on the table and mixed like cement, but a bowl seems easier and works as well). Mix with a wooden spoon, then knead with your fingers till it is a nice bungy compact ball – a minute or less is quite enough. Put it into a plastic bag previously smeared on the inside with margarine, and leave to rise in a warm place for an hour or two.

When ready, preheat the oven to gas mark 7 (425° F, 220° C). Roll out the dough on a floured board to the approximate shape of your pizza dish, which you have previously greased or oiled (an ordinary baking dish is all right), pushing it into the corners and edges with your fingers so it just fits. Spread tomato sauce all over it, and place sliced tomatoes, strips of ham, grated Cheddar cheese (when in Italy use mozzarella), a sprinkling of oil and anything else the family likes, on top. Bake about 30–40 minutes.

Tomato Sauce

2–3 tablespoons olive oil   Fresh or dried basil
1 medium tin tomatoes   1 teaspoon sugar
5–6 cloves garlic, peeled   Salt, pepper

Put the oil into a frying pan and heat briefly. Then add the whole tin of tomatoes, the garlic (whole), a handful of basil, chopped a little, the sugar, salt and pepper. Cook moderately, stirring with a wooden spoon and making sure it doesn't burn, until it looks like a sauce. Remove garlic if you don't like chewing it.

Vanessa Thomas

The Longleat Picnic

CHRISTOPHER THYNNE

Sun is sinking, cars are loaded
Children, food and frying pans,
A basket full of drink and tumblers,
Lemonade and Cola cans.

Dogs are barking, parents shouting,
Dressed in jeans and tweedy suits,
'Have we got a bottle opener?
Sophie, you've forgot your boots.'

The cavalcade of cars starts rolling,
Someone shouts, 'Who's got the pugs?'
Silvy runs back from the Mill House
Loaded with a pile of rugs.

Start again, out through the driveway,
Swirling dust clouds in our wake,
Down the lane and through the woodland,
Heading for the Island Lake.

I love the sound and smell of cooking,
Everybody's had a drink,
One or two are on their second,
Ed is on his third, I think.

Alexander's acting strangely,
Think he's getting rather tight.
Now he's dancing like a dervish,
Someone's set his beard alight.

Tony's chatting up the Duchess.
I think he sometimes goes too far.
The fire's burning rather well now,
Think I'll strum on my guitar.

I'm sure I put it here beside me.
Now it's vanished from my sight.
Oh my God – some stupid bugger,
So that's why the fire's so bright.

Christ! It's getting rather cold now,
Wish that I was in my car,
Put my coat on, pick up litter,
Throw some wood on my guitar.

Time to go now – what a pity,
Just as things were going well,
Life's a picnic – earth's a heaven,
Both to me just now are hell.

Grope our way back through the darkness,
Tree Trunk Bridge I see, I think.
What's that splash? Dad's in the water –
That's goodbye to all the drink.

Matches flare and fade like fireflies,
Someone's fallen in the stream,
Voices calling all around me,
Havoc's reigning quite supreme.

What the hell? – I think I'll stay here,
Wrap up warm – I'll be all right,
I'd only fall into the water –
We're coming back tomorrow night.

A Dorsetshire Picnic

TANYA VINOGRADOFF

One of our favourite picnicking places is a great circular wood of ancient yew trees on the Downs. The branches join together overhead to make a dim cathedral gloom. The floor is neatly covered with pine needles, perfect for lighting a fire, and in the middle of the wood is a sunny, grassy glade. Here one needs plenty of rugs, mackintoshes or groundsheets for damp ground; shady hats; and plenty of good baskets for carrying food and drink easily. I am a great collector of baskets of all kinds. I have a very good French one, divided into four for carrying bottles and thermoses; another from Burgos has a lid like Red Riding Hood's basket; and I also possess a big Chinese basket, like a suitcase, which has to be carried flat, will hold food as well as plates, and is more useful than a fitted basket. I think all picnic food should be eatable either with fingers or with a fork. Once you have to cut things with a knife you need a table, and then you might just as well be at home on your terrace.

All the food should be simple and fresh, not too rich, full of herbs and piquant tastes, plenty of chives, tarragon and basil. As with all food, presentation and colour are important – the bright green of parsley and watercress, the palest green of cucumber and celery, the red of tomatoes and radishes. Nothing greasy and no soggy sandwiches.

Omelette in a Long Loaf

4 eggs

Chopped spring onions, chives, parsley, tarragon

Salt, pepper

Butter

1 long loaf

Beat up the eggs with the seasoning and herbs so that the mixture looks quite green. Meanwhile cut a long loaf in half lengthways. Take out some of the crumb and butter both sides. Cook the omelette so that it is rather firm, and roll it into the shape of the loaf. Place on the bottom half of the loaf, put the 'lid' on, wrap in foil and put a weight on the top. This will then slice into neat slices when needed.

Kotelettes Pojarski

1 veal chop per person

4 oz (110 g) white breadcrumbs

Milk

Butter and oil for frying

Soak the breadcrumbs in milk, then squeeze them out. Trim the veal and chop finely. Mix with the breadcrumbs and shape into flat round cakes. Fry quickly in half oil, half butter until brown. Reduce the heat and cook for 20 minutes. Drain and serve with a sharp tomato sauce if liked. These are nice hot or cold.

Rich Ginger Cake

This must be made a day or two beforehand.

4 oz (110 g) butter

4 oz (110 g) sugar

4 oz (110 g) sultanas

10 oz (275 g) black treacle

1 teaspoon ground ginger

2 eggs

8 oz (220 g) plain flour

Preheat the oven to gas mark 4 (350° F, 180° C). Cream the butter, add the sugar, and cream again thoroughly. Add the fruit, treacle, ginger and the eggs one at a time with half of the flour. Mix thoroughly. Add the remaining flour. Turn at once into a greased and floured tin and bake for an hour or more.

Tanya Vinogradoff —

Dominican Picnic

MARGARET VYNER

Dominica, lying between Martinique and Guadeloupe, unloved by many tourists for its black beaches and incessant rain, brought back childhood memories of my grandfather's Victorian conservatory with the smell of damp and warmth and faintly rotting vegetation. The hotel where we stayed was deep in the hilly rain forest. When we arrived it was nearly empty but we were intrigued to find on a notice board a mysterious small card advertising 'DOMINICA SAFARIS', which promised a drive round the island followed by a picnic beside a river where we could swim; so, not knowing what to expect, we booked in. On the appointed morning a brand-new sand-coloured Range Rover appeared, driven by a handsome, bearded West Indian in a matching sand-coloured safari suit and an Ernest Hemingway hat; and as we set off we felt that had it been cold he would have tucked a rug round our knees.

The drive itself was breathtaking: in spite of the word safari, we saw nothing but vegetation of such enormity and density that at any moment a Douanier Rousseau tiger might have appeared. We arrived eventually on the site of our picnic: huge rocks, huge ferns and a fast-flowing icy-cold clear river and not a soul in sight. Our driver said that while we swam he would lay out the picnic. When we emerged, starving and half expecting sandwiches and bananas, we were astonished by what we saw. Spread out on a white damask cloth straight from an Edwardian shooting party was the most ravishing and delicious feast imaginable.

First of all, we were given ice-cold rum punches in crystal glasses, and while we sat on the rocks drinking them we gazed greedily at what was to come: stuffed crabs, exotic chicken, avocado mousse, sweet potato bread and mango ice cream. Euphoric after our rum punches (particularly delicious as the Dominican rum and limes are famously good) we set to, and it all tasted as wonderful as it looked, especially as the driver produced a bottle of Clos des Mouches tasting of primroses. Like all good picnics, it seemed to go on for hours, and the experience of enjoying wonderful food and drink in a jungle setting – ferns, plantains, the warm damp air and the only sound (apart from sighs of gluttonous pleasure) that of the running river – was unforgettable.

Two years later we came back to Dominica longing to repeat the experience, but we looked in vain for the card at the hotel, asked in vain about Dominica Safaris, and were met with blank black faces – it seemed not so much to have vanished without trace as never to have existed: it had been a *Marie Celeste* of picnics.

Stuffed Crabs

Land crabs are used on the island for this first-course dish.

6 small hard-shell crabs
3 oz (75 g) freshly made
  breadcrumbs
1 fresh hot pepper, seeded and
  chopped fine, or hot pepper
  sauce to taste
3 tablespoons chopped chives
2 tablespoons chopped parsley

2 cloves garlic, crushed
1 tablespoon fresh lime juice
Salt and freshly ground pepper
¼ teaspoon allspice
3 tablespoons Madeira or dark
  rum, preferably Martinique
  or Guadeloupe *rhum vieux*
Butter

Preheat the oven to gas mark 4 (350° F, 180° C). Plunge the crabs into boiling water and boil for 8–10 minutes. Remove and cool. Take out the meat from the shells and claws and chop it finely. Discard the spongy fibre. Scrub out the empty shells, if small, and reserve. Mash 2 oz (50 g) of breadcrumbs into the crabmeat until the mixture is quite smooth. Add the hot pepper, chives, parsley, lime juice, salt, pepper, allspice, Madeira or rum, mixing thoroughly. Stuff the reserved crab shells with the mixture. If using three or four larger crabs, use the meat to stuff six scallop shells or put in ramekins.

Sprinkle with the remaining breadcrumbs and dot with butter. Bake for 30 minutes, or until lightly browned.

If live crabs are not available, buy 1 lb (450 g) of fresh, frozen or tinned crabmeat, or buy plain boiled crabs.

Chicken Calypso
(serves six)

5 tablespoons olive oil
4 lb (1 kg 800 g) chicken, cut
 into serving pieces
1 lb 2 oz (500 g) rice
1 medium onion, finely chopped
1 clove garlic, chopped
1 green bell pepper, seeded
 and chopped
1 small hot green pepper,
 seeded and chopped

8 oz (225 g) mushrooms, sliced
½ teaspoon saffron
Piece of lime peel
1 tablespoon lime juice
¼ teaspoon Angostura bitters
2 pints (1 litre 140 ml)
 chicken stock
Salt
Freshly ground pepper
3 tablespoons light rum

Heat 3 tablespoons of the oil in a skillet and sauté the chicken pieces until brown all over. Remove to a heavy casserole. Add the rice, onion, garlic, bell pepper and hot pepper to the oil remaining in the skillet and sauté, stirring until the oil is absorbed, being careful not to let the rice scorch. Add to the chicken in the casserole. Add the remaining 2 tablespoons of oil to the skillet, and sauté the mushrooms over a fairly high heat for 5 minutes. Add to the casserole with the saffron, lime peel, lime juice, bitters, stock and salt and pepper to taste. Cover and simmer gently until the rice and chicken are tender and the liquid absorbed – about 30 minutes. Add the rum and cook uncovered for 5 minutes longer.

Hartley Augiste's Rum Punch
(serves one)

2 fl. oz (55 ml) Dominica
 rum or light rum from
 Martinique or Guadeloupe
½ fl. oz (15 ml) lime
 juice

3 teaspoons simple syrup
 (see below)
2–3 dashes Angostura bitters
3–4 ice cubes
Maraschino cherry

Combine ingredients in a cocktail shaker and shake hard. Strain over ice cubes.

Simple Syrup

1 lb (450 g) granulated sugar
¾ pint (425 ml) cold water

Combine the two in a bowl and stir from time to time until dissolved. Use in drinks instead of sugar. 1 tablespoon of syrup = 1½ teaspoons of sugar

Mango Ice Cream

4 eggs
4 oz (110 g) sugar
¾ pint (425 ml) milk
1 cup of mango pulp mixed with 2 oz (50 g) sugar
  (extra to above)
½ teaspoon vanilla essence

Beat the eggs lightly with the sugar. Scald the milk and stir into the eggs. Cook the egg mixture on top of a double boiler over hot water, stirring constantly until the mixture coats the spoon. Cool and add mango pulp. Freeze to a mush. Remove from the refrigerator and beat well. Freeze again.

A Picnic in the Grand Manner

FRANCIS WATSON

Personally, I confess that I avoid picnics as far as possible. But I must say that I should have rather liked to attend one of Sir Richard Wallace's shooting picnics, like that in the Great Wood at Sudbourn Hall shown in the picture, dated 1876, by the forgotten French artist Alfred-Charles-Ferdinand Decaen.

The Sudbourn estate in Suffolk was one of the entailed Hertford properties and so did not pass to Sir Richard Wallace under his father's will. But in order to relieve the fifth Marquis from what would have been a burden to maintain after the loss of the Irish estates and the bulk of the huge Hertford fortune, Wallace purchased it from him for the then very considerable sum of £200,000 – much, it is recorded, to the heir's relief.

Sudbourn Hall has disappeared today – it was demolished in the 1950s, but there is an excellent account of it in *Another Part of the Wood*, the first volume of the memoirs of Lord Clark, who spent much of his early childhood there. During the fourth Lord Hertford's lifetime the estate had been neglected. He had no interest in country pursuits and, in any case, hardly ever left Paris for any of his nine homes in England. His father, the third Marquis (and Thackeray's model for Lord Steyne) had greatly enjoyed the shooting there and kept the estate well stocked with partridges. Wallace restocked it with game after 1871 and kept it up in high state until he finally left England in 1886. He had twenty-three gamekeepers, and on most weekends in the autumn there were at least six guns staying in the house (often French friends from Paris), and neighbours were regularly invited over for a day's shooting. Edward VII, as Prince of Wales, stayed at Sudbourn on a number of occasions, and on one at least confided to his private diary his sufferings at having the tongue-tied Lady Wallace as his neighbour at dinner ('. . . fortunately Lady Wallace had a headache this evening and did not come down to dinner . . .'). The Prince was not alone in his opinion of his hostess. A Suffolk neighbour, the first Earl of Cranbrook, came to shoot in November 1872 and commented subsequently: 'The dinner was too good and required care and firmness. Lady Wallace speaks only French, and I took her in, to my dismay, and stumbled through some very bad language.'

If the dinners were 'too good', the al fresco shooting lunches seem to have been anything but spartan. Decaen's painting shows trestle tables, linen tablecloths and comfortable chairs to avoid that great disadvantage of most picnics, the discomfort of having to eat sitting on damp grass. The long table is properly laid with silver, though not Sir Richard's best, for he possessed wonderful French silver both of the eighteenth century and the Empire period, though these were not amongst the works of art bequeathed by his widow to the British nation, since it was regarded as of merely utilitarian value, and only 'works of art' were included in Lady Wallace's bequest. When I first went to the Wallace Collection, some members of the staff still recalled that it took four workmen an entire week to remove the contents of the silver vaults from Manchester Square to nearby Connaught Square where Sir John Murray Scott, the heir, had his house.

At the moment chosen by the artist the picnic has not yet begun. Luncheon has clearly been delayed for the arrival of Lady Wallace, who is seen at the left of the painting being handed down from her victoria by her son, Captain Edmund Wallace, whilst Henry Grimwood, the head groom, holds the horses' heads. Her companion on the brief journey from the Hall has already alighted and is quite evidently a Frenchwoman. She is in all probability the Comtesse d'Armaillé, wife of the well-known Parisian art collector whose letters are our main source of information about the Wallaces' shooting parties, at which the French couple were regular visitors. It seems likely, too, that her husband is the gentleman standing close by Madame d'Armaillé. His shooting costume seems rather more continental in cut than those of Wallace's English friends gathered around the lunch table. No doubt Lady Wallace found them a good deal easier to converse with than Suffolk landowners. Wallace himself seems to have reached the spot only moments before his wife's arrival. He can be seen at the centre of the painting where his valet is helping him to remove a fur-lined ulster of a somewhat Parisian design.

Unhappily, the main dishes have not yet been served, but their quality may probably be judged by the large *foie gras de Strasbourg en croûte* that the butler is carving at an improvised sideboard on the extreme right of the picture. The numerous wine bottles already on the table, as well as the large silver wine cooler, add to the impression that the quality of the food was well above what most of us are accustomed to at picnics. In the foreground a footman is quenching the thirst of a retriever from a wine bottle. Did it contain only water? In another painting from the same series, another footman is using Perrier water for a similar purpose.

Doubtless the afternoon's *battue* was as well organized as the picnic, for Wallace kept the estate well stocked. No game card for this particular weekend survives, but I have before me as I write such a card for December of the following year. Many of the guests were present on both occasions. At that six-day party no less than 4116 head of game were slaughtered.

A memorable picnic indeed.

Francis Watson

A Spontini Picnic

WILLIAM WEAVER

I love music and I love food. Normally I do not enjoy them together. I have walked out of restaurants in protest (ineffectual, I fear) against their Muzak or their pianist; I have asked hostesses to turn off the radio or the gramophone; and it is years since I have picnicked on a beach, because the invasion of transistors has succeeded in spoiling that pleasure. So naturally, on a picnic, I would ban any kind of music, reproduced or live (the sight of a guitar immediately suggests the drawl of folk songs and, just as immediately, provokes anticipatory indigestion).

Still, I must admit that one of the most enjoyable al frescos I have had was, in fact, a musical evening on my own terrace. It was several years ago, and Italian Radio was broadcasting *Agnes Von Hohenstausen*, a rarely performed opera by Spontini, starring Monserrat Caballe. I learned about the broadcast only after I had invited a few friends to supper.

Fortunately the guests were all music lovers and, in fact, as eager to hear the opera as I was. The radio, however, and the taping equipment were in my cluttered study, which was not the ideal room for dining in. But just outside the study window there is a terrace, with a pergola of grapevines, a table and some chairs. The loudspeakers in the study could be shifted to the window, so that they could be heard by listeners on the terrace. The food, which was cold, had been prepared in the afternoon. It was placed on the table so that guests could help themselves, and they were asked to be on hand a good half hour before the opera was about to begin. So we had time for a glass of wine. After the music started the only noise was an occasional gurgle of more wine being poured and perhaps one or two clanks of dropped cutlery. There were long intervals between the acts, so we could enjoy more talk. And then, when it was over, we had a final glass and exchanged impressions.

We ate one of the many Italian kinds of cold pasta (which I know sounds revolting to the Anglo-Saxon, but is actually delicious), a cold *frittata* – by cold I mean room-temperature – and a salad and cheeses and fruit (perhaps grapes from above our heads). And, to be sure, Spontini. Just the right composer for a Tuscan picnic. Verdi would have demanded our total attention, distracting us from the food; and perhaps another composer – I'll name no names – would not have prevented us from talking.

Cold Chitarrucci

1 lb (450 g) pasta (if possible chitarrucci – the squared
 off fine spaghetti)
2 lb (900 g) tomatoes
1 cup full of basil and marjoram, finely chopped
Salt, pepper
Olive oil

Prepare the sauce one day before. Peel, seed and chop the tomatoes. Put in a bowl and add the chopped marjoram, basil, plenty of salt and pepper. Leave it to sweat. Drain. Add the oil.

Next day, cook the pasta in the ordinary way. Cool by tossing well in the sauce.

Frittata

½ glass olive oil
Small onion
2 large tomatoes, peeled
 and chopped
1 lb (450 g) courgettes,
 chopped

Salt, pepper
8 eggs
1 tablespoon flour
1 tablespoon grated Parmesan
6–7 leaves basil, chopped
6–7 leaves celery, chopped

Chop the onion and fry gently. Add the tomatoes and courgettes. Cook on a high heat for about 20 minutes in a frying pan. Mix the eggs with the cheese, flour, salt and pepper. When the courgettes are cooked take them off the heat and add to the egg mixture. Stir quickly. Add the basil and celery leaves. Put back on a high heat and cook on both sides, turning with the help of a plate. Cool. If the frittata breaks, beat another egg and use for repair work.

William Weaver

A Boer Picnic

GEOFFREY WHEATCROFT

Halfway up the hill we stalled. The big Ford truck, like a larger Land Rover, was almost bogged down in the sand before we rolled back and took a faster run at it. When we made the crest there were two miraculous views. Behind us was the valley. In among the violent shadows cast by the setting sun, mixed ochres were broken by pastel patches of scrub. In the distance were the ruins of the ghost town we had driven through. At the turn of the century, when Namibia was German South-West Africa, it had been a mining town and a rail-head. Then the copper ran out and it reverted to wilderness. Ahead of us stretched a flat plateau of desert, dappled by the sunset. As we drove across it pairs of gemsbok and oryx scurried in the distance.

Our destination would have been hard to find as a map reference. The driver knew the way. Camp – of a sort – had been pitched in a little hollow, sheltered on one side by an outcrop of rocks. They had put up a three-sided canvas wall with a partition. On one side of it were a couple of dozen beds. We were to sleep in the open, looking up at the stars. In theory this is safe if there is a rubber groundsheet under the bottom sheet of the bed; the fact is that a heavy dew soaks through the bedding. You can wake, as I woke, with a sore throat and an aching back; although, as someone said, they may have been caused as much by the previous evening as by the night.

A trench had been dug for the *braaivleis* (Afrikaner barbecue), and the wood was already burning down. Where the wood had come from was something of a mystery although there were small trees, more like bushes, here and there.

The sight of the trestle table prompted the jokester of the party: there must have been more liquid reposing on it than in all the watercourses of the Namib desert. There was every known kind of spirit, including a particularly lethal Cape brandy, there was wine, and there was Hansa, the local beer brewed in Swakopmund. In Johannesburg I had grown fond of Hansa, but it is much the same as the beers in every tropical or sub-tropical country. It is rather sweet and fizzy, only tolerable if very cold. This beer *was* cold. It had been brought across the desert in ice boxes.

It was a long wait before dinner. There was some biltong to nibble, strips of wind-dried beef as chewy as toffee, an acquired taste. And there was *boerewors* – 'farmer's sausage' – already grilled. We talked about the day before, and another *braai* the previous evening in Arandis. The grill was covered now with crayfish split open (they must have been brought up to the desert on ice, too), and little titbits rolled in bacon, and fillet steak, not in large pieces but cut into delicate tournedos.

Sentimental delusion plays a part in picnics. We persuade ourselves that, because we are eating something not very nice in decidedly uncomfortable surroundings, we must be enjoying ourselves. This was different. The grilled crayfish really were better than the *Homard rôti et fumé dans la cheminée*, which I had eaten a few weeks before in one of the most famous (and certainly one of the most expensive) restaurants in France. And the steaks were at least as good as in any London restaurant. It was the best meal I had eaten in nearly two months in southern Africa, although that is not a high standard of comparison.

Before dinner we drank more beer – there had been a bottle or two coming across the desert – and for those who wanted gin or whisky there was as much ice as they liked. The two important things about picnic drink are that there should be a lot of it and that it should be cold. How did picnickers manage before cheap ice and thermos flasks and insulated bags? Two centuries ago, rich landowners could have raided their ingenious ice stores if they wanted cool drinks for an al fresco meal. Other people must have drunk their beer lukewarm – a depressing thought.

There was cold wine, too, with the crayfish, a good South African white called Simonsig Kerner, and a red as well. After dinner we talked and drank and sang until late into the night. Our hosts had a rather blunt idea of how to make the party go with a swing. 'When

we've finished this song everyone will tell the dirtiest joke he knows.'
As this was said I was watching the fastidious Viennese who repre-
sents a famous German paper in Johannesburg, and saw a spasm
of pain cross his face. The best I could do was to sing an Irish song,
with a fixed grin. Whatever time it was when we went to bed, it was
too late.

The damp beds did us no good, as I have said, and few of us felt like
sightseeing the next day. The sights on offer were exotic. There were
more breathtakingly beautiful gazelles and there was a two-
thousand-year-old tree, growing on its own in the middle of the
desert, far out of sight of any other vegetation. At lunchtime we were
driven back to the airstrip to say goodbye and fly to Windhoek. Our
three days had been fun – interesting rather than joyful – and the
braai was the best part of it. But there was something wrong. Our
hosts should have been hunters or farmers, people who knew the
countryside of that remote, beautiful and empty land: as it was, we
had been entertained so generously by the company that owns the
biggest uranium mine in the world.

Geoffrey Wheatcroft

Recipe Index